HIGHLAND WAYS AND BYWAYS

CULLERNIE CRAFTS
in association with
CLUB LEABHAR LIMITED

IN MEMORIAM: Coinneach Mor

'Togaidh an obair an fhianuis'

HIGHLAND WAYS AND BYWAYS

A Selection from the writings of

KENNETH A. MACRAE
'Coinneach Mor'

CULLERNIE CRAFTS
in association with
CLUB LEABHAR LIMITED

SBN 902706 26 8

The extracts in this book have been taken from:
Highland Doorstep, 1953; Highland Handshake, 1954;
and Northern Narrative, 1955

Published in Scotland by Cullernie Crafts and distributed by
Club Leabhar Limited, Inverness IV1 2HJ

Printed in the Highlands of Scotland by
John G. Eccles, Henderson Road, Inverness

It was a double pleasure, tinged with regret, which I experienced when asked to make some extracts from the works of Coinneach Mor. The regret was that the author had died in 1972, at no great age for a man, and was thus not able to enjoy again the fruits of his earlier labours. The three books from which these extracts are taken were truly revealing in that they exposed both the country in the Inverness hinterland and its people — to be revealed in a new and sympathetic light: thirled to the land and loving it by preserving all its worthy past. Ken Macrae was no armchair traveller. He shod himself with his best pair of walking boots and roamed the highways and byways of the countryside, meeting people on their own doorsteps and making fast friends with many of them. That he succeeded in dismantling the usual reserve of the folk he met is seen in his excellent works and the many articles he wrote for newspapers and magazines after 1955, when his last book appeared.

The two pleasures mentioned above refer to the fresh acquaintance I made with Ken's books and the thought that I was in some small way instrumental in bringing them once more to the notice of a new reading public. The originals are now out of print, but keep cropping up, though not regularly, in the lists of second-hand booksellers.

Inevitably, in the time since the first book was published, 'Highland Doorstep,' in 1953, many things have changed. Many of the people whom Ken met in his travels are now gone. Even buildings have either disappeared or have had their uses changed from residential to factory. What has been preserved from the three books is the essence of the folk history of the area round about Inverness, the Black Isle, north to Beauly and Dingwall, in the area of the Great Glen, and round about Strathnairn. Insofar as few books deal with the local history of these parts, this present volume will serve a useful function as a guide book, not only to the casual tourist, but to those who are newly arrived to live in the Moray Firth area, and also to those who, though native to the place, have perhaps never had the time to investigate their indigenous landscape, environment, heritage and background. If this book serves to impart a small measure of appreciation of the countryside to all of these, then it will have served its purpose well and proved that good original writing has a unique staying power and, in this present instance, indicated that Coinneach Mor has a permanent place in the corpus of Highland literature.

Francis Thompson,
Baile Loch,
Siorrachd Inbhirnis   An t-Sultain, 1973

Contents

1. CEUD MILLE FAILTE

All roads lead to Rome! That's a well-known adage in everyday use.
But if we glance for a moment at a map of the North of Scotland,
with the Highland Capital as a central point, we might easily claim
that "all roads lead to Inverness!" On the eastern side of the town we
find a definite arterial net-work of roads branching in all directions;
at least half a dozen of them. Of these, five will be described in the
ensuing pages; the sixth, taking the traveller into the Nairn district,
will later be included in our wanderings around the Moray Firth.

On all town boundaries we may find on a notice board the
Inverness coat of arms surmounted with the words *Ceud Mile Failte*,
and the name of Inverness printed below. It is, indeed, a true
Highland welcome: "A Hundred Thousand Welcomes!"

Coming in from the south road, especially, it gives you a feeling of
warmth to find that you are going in among friends; that you are
welcome. The journey from the south may have been tiresome and
even monotonous over long stretches of moorland and heather, and
as you come within sight of chimney stacks you are greeted at the
gateway. A Hundred Thousand Welcomes — to civilisation!

But wait! How inconsiderate you can be! How ignorant! Behind
you lies a land unknown, full of romance and glory. Full of kindly
country folk who can extend a welcome to you, second to none; as I
have verily found out for myself in a series of visits to their own
firesides, to hear the lore and see their way of life at present and in
days gone by.

Culcabock marks the boundary of the Highland Capital on the
Great North Road leading south, and, before ascending the brae,
which takes us up into the heights of Drummossie, we pass through
the lands of Inshes.

Across the road from Inshes, the house of Castlehill is almost
hidden behind a high wall, and in a corner of the old walled garden
lie the remains of one, James Grant, of the Shewglie family
(Glenurquhart), who was sent by Grant of Shewglie to Prince Charlie
with a message of welcome at the time of the '45. He joined the
Prince's army and accompanied him to Derby, and was with him
during the retreat as far as Culloden, where he fell fatally wounded.
Yet he managed to struggle to his aunt's home at Castlehill, where
he died within a few hours of reaching it.

The Prince is believed to have halted at Castlehill for two nights on his way to Inverness; and also associated with the old house is the famous Colbert, minister to Louis XIV of France, whose grandfather was a Cuthbert of Castlehill, a well-known family in the 16th and 17th centuries.

The House of Inshes (Gaelic, *Innis* — a choice pasture), like Castlehill, is pre-Culloden, and has been associated with a family of Robertsons for generations. In fact, the last of this family, a descendent of the Robertsons of Struan, chiefs of their clan, sold the estate, and latterly lived at Culcabock House, where he died within living memory.

I am told that the old well at the roadside at Culcabock has been wrongly associated with King Duncan, and that it was actually named after a Duncan Robertson of Inshes, and has nothing whatsoever to do with this Scottish King!

The families of Baird, MacKintosh, and the late Lord Gough are the more recent owners of Inshes House; Lord Gough was a direct descendant of the victor of Chillian Walla, a battle of the Sikh War, fought over a hundred years ago.

Many old houses boast a ghost, and Inshes is no exception. I have not heard of the little "brown-suited Robertson" apparition being seen in recent years, but Mrs Lilian Hartley, herself a MacKintosh by birth, recalled some of the uncanny happenings of her youth spent at Inshes.

"I remember, on one occasion, my brother wakened me in the middle of the night to ask if I heard a terrible noise up in the attics of the house," she told me. "He had been awake for quite a while listening to it, and when I heard it too, I agreed that it was the most terrible noise of the kind to which I had ever listened. Of course, we knew nobody was there, which didn't console us in the least.

"Another time, my mother's maid, Jessie Grant, had been making the beds with one of the housemaids, and on her way to the bedrooms had to step aside in the passage to let the little man pass, but I don't believe the other girl even saw him!"

Whoever the little man was in actual life is rather a mystery, but one thing is sure — he liked his dram.

"So much so," said Mrs Hartley, "that his wife shut him up in the attic with a barrel of whisky, and there he stayed until it was finished. Somehow he escaped, and fell headlong down the stairs and broke his neck. My sister saw his ghost falling down the attic stairs on several occasions!"

An old dove-cot at the rear of Inshes House, I believe, dates back to 1463, and along with another, now out of existence, was originally used as a lookout post against invading enemies. Another interesting relic is a 400-year-old ash tree, standing beside the house.

Perhaps the most interesting parish south-east of Inverness is Daviot, stretching from Wester Aberchalder to Culloden Moor, and including the famous battlefield. It was formed by the union of a smaller Daviot parish and Dunlichity in 1618.

The village of Daviot is a somewhat scattered community, divided by the valley of the River Nairn, and, long ago, famines were prevalent in this district, due mostly to the land being insufficiently cultivated. Bad drainage also made the neighbourhood peculiarly liable to mildew in autumn, so that between the two evils the people were in a pretty bad way. A single morning of frost in August or September might easily dash the hopes of a farmer for the season. One famine proved so severe that only two brothers survived in the Gask and Faillie area.

Having climbed to a considerable altitude after leaving the Highland Capital, the road levels out over Bogbain Moor, but inevitably takes a dip down to the level of the River Nairn, and then begins another climb, with a hairpin bend at the foot of it. It is in this slow descent from moor and heather that we find Daviot sheltering in the lap of Dun Davie.

The old kirk of Daviot lies on our left, but hidden in some trees north of it is the manse.

Dun Davie hill is presumably the site of an old fort, but in more recent years has formed a source of local employment as a whinstone quarry.

At the roadside on the south slope rising from the river valley, Craggie Inn was a popular landmark with travellers, but the last licensee, the late Peter MacKenzie, went to Canada about 1911. So now the wayfarer has to rely on hotels for a "drink for the road," and one such place is the Meallmore Hotel, originally a shooting lodge, but now converted into an hotel.

2. DARK DEEDS

I never saw Strathnairn on a really fine day, but that does not necessarily mean that this bonnie Inverness-shire Strath is proverbially wet. Not at all. I believe in summer it is ideal. Perhaps its charm and Highland tranquility have much to do with the choice of H.R.H. the Duke of Gloucester, who took a ten year lease of the Farr Estate as a holiday home.

I only made three visits to Strathnairn, and on these brief occasions found many places of interest. I met the country people, mostly crofters, but it was the older folk who were able to recall the tales their mothers told them of the Strath they had come to call their home.

There are more than half a dozen ways to enter Strathnairn: by Daviot; the Old Edinburgh Road; Culduthel Road; Essich; Stratherrick; and all the small byways.

The entry from Daviot is two-fold; either past the school and below Dun Davie, or by turning to the right when travelling south at the War Memorial, near the local police station. I took the latter byway, and made Lairgindour my first port of call.

Lairgindour lies above the road on the crest of a hill and was formerly on the Meallmore Estate.

The Mains of Gask, a farm on the Inverernie estate, lies to the east of Culduthel road from Inverness on the edge of Strathnairn. I remember going to a displenishing sale there several years ago and purchasing an old sledge, which had been used previously for feeding sheep with turnips in winter, but had originally been discarded from Moy Hall. Who knows, even royalty may have travelled in it! It was knocked down to me for ten shillings, and has since been used in a fancy dress parade, coming through it with honours!

At the time of Culloden, Gask Mains was tenanted by a famous cattle dealer, John MacGillivray, whose brother, Alex. MacGillivray of Dunmaglass, commanded the MacKintosh clan at the battle. In his day, John was widely known as "Big John of the Markets," and although presumed killed at Culloden, he escaped and went to America, where he became a Colonel in a Royalist Regiment in the American War of Independence. It is a tradition that during the Battle of Culloden he killed fourteen men with his broad sword, and probably a great many more.

From the roadside you can see the complete Stone Circles, vestiges of Druid times, standing on a slight hillock on the farm land of Gask, and it was here that the Clan MacGillivray representatives at Culloden halted on the way to the battle, and sharpened their broad swords and dirks on the largest of the stones. In fact, the marks on the surface can still be seen.

At the same time they stopped for refreshment and ate oatcakes and cheese, washed down with a dram! Then on they went to the fight, many of them, including their leader, to meet their deaths.

Leaving Gask Mains, the high road from Daviot crosses one's path at Balnafoich, and, passing by Beachan and Achvaneran, I came to the humpy-back bridge at Tordarroch, centuries old, and only touched up on the walls with cement for preservation. As I crossed it in my car, with little room to spare on either side, I thought of the changes this very bridge had seen in its day. Prince Charlie, escaping from Culloden, had ridden over it to reach his friend, Shaw, at Tordarroch House, but had found the house empty. Some say he was hiding in the attic, but maybe that is merely conjecture.

In those days Tordarroch was a three-storeyed mansion house, belonging to a family of Shaws.

It is doubtful whether the present farmhouse at Tordarroch is part of the old mansion house. In an overgrown pond nearby, I understand relics of by-gone clan feuds were found long ago, and her father once made the unusual discovery of a Wellington boot — with a leg in it! It caused quite a stir in the community and was sent up to Inverness for investigation, but nothing more was heard about it.

In the year 1530, the barn of Tordarroch was the scene of rather a bloody massacre. It all started over a clan chiefship dispute between the Earl of Moray, acting on behalf of young MacKintosh, then not "of age," and Hector MacKintosh of MacKintosh. A meeting was called by the Earl of Moray to settle the dispute, and when his opponent's followers turned up for the gathering, eighteen of them were strung up from the rafters, giving rise to an old saying from the chance remark of one who was there:

"It's not every day that MacKintosh holds a court"!

These are the facts contained in the History of the Clan Chattan, but local lore has a slightly different version. Finlay Smith, Achvaneran, was the first to tell me that the actual number killed was fifty, and not eighteen, and many others endorsed his story.

"They were buried in Dunlichity Churchyard," said Finlay. "I believe that name comes from the Gaelic *Dun-lechead,* and means the heap of the half hundred."

However, there may have been a clan battle nearby to account for the name.

Gaelic scholars I have approached have other ideas, and my friend, the late John N. Macleod, thought it more probable that both Dunlichity and Flichity are derived from the Gaelic, meaning "A wet hill."

One of the MacQueen family in the district was responsible for the killing of a wolf, which had been doing great damage among the flocks of Strathdearn sometime about 1730.

The story goes that The Mackintosh called together all the folk of Strathdearn he could muster to help drive the hills at Polochaig, and that MacQueen, being late for the gathering, was severely reprimanded by the Chief. But no one was more astonished than the MacKintosh when MacQueen produced the wolf's head from under his plaid. He had met the wolf on the way over and had killed it!

In the old days he used to ring the hand bell, inscribed "Robert Mcconache 1702," to bring the folk to Church. The bell now rests in a corner cupboard of the vestry, and has an interesting story attached to it.

When plans were made to build the Church at Dunlichity, the bell was taken there. It re-appeared, however, at Brinmore, some three miles away, now only the site of the former Church. Some folk thought that supernatural powers were at work, because every time it was taken to Dunlichity it re-appeared next day at Brinmore!

The Church built at Dunlichity in 1759 was the third to be placed on that site. A tradition says that a former building had a porch, where the men of the district left their bows and arrows during the services, and the marks of the sharpening of the arrows were seen on the porch door. Actually on the east gable end of the present Church you can see these marks.

Another interesting old stone tells rather a remarkable tale in itself — provided the facts carved on it are authentic and not merely a "printer's error."

It is to the memory of Alexander MacGillivray of Dalcrombie, who died on the 18th January, 1797, aged 38. Also his son, Donald MacGillivray, who died 18th September, 1797, aged 25.

That means the son was born when his father was only thirteen years old!

"He must hae been mairrit awfy young!" commented my guide.

At the corner of the churchyard is the old watch-tower, from where relatives of newly-interred corpses watched their graves against body-snatchers, and on one particular tombstone I saw marks of gun pellets, which surely must have made the vultures step lively on that occasion.

Beside a small burn about a hundred yards away, a moss covered stone recalls memories of by-gone baptisms. The centre of the stone is hollowed out, and I am told all babies born in the district were christened by the burn side.

Over a century ago an old meal mill stood in a field opposite Dunlichity Churchyard on the glebe ground, and in nearby Loch Chlachlain lies an ancient millstone, which never even reached its destination at the mill. It had been hewn out of rock on the hillside overlooking the loch, and rolled down some fifty yards, when it got out of control and finished its passage at the foot of the loch. I believe it can be seen lying at the bottom on a clear day, but nobody has managed yet to retrieve it!

The rocky nature of the ground, due to glacial action, is peculiar to Strathnairn, and on *Creag a Chlachain,* behind the Church a hoof print of a horse on the bare rock was discovered. But no one has ever ascertained how it happened to get there!

On another rocky hillside, to the west of Loch Duntelchaig, lie the empty buildings of Letterchullin, where one of the last wolves in Scotland was killed by a woman with a girdle in her hand. She had gone to Letterchullin from Dunchea, in Stratherrick, to borrow the girdle, met the wolf on her homeward journey, and consequently crowned it in self-defence!

The village of Farr is scattered, and besides the Free Kirk, school and post office, has few other houses.

Flichity Inn has little connection with Flichity itself, and was formerly known as Tighanallan. It is not very old, being built about 1860 by a Mr Sutherland Walker, who was also responsible for Brin House and some of the buildings in nearby East Croachy.

Brin House itself is a splendid building made of coloured granite, although no known quarry of this stone exists anywhere in the neighbourhood.

Brin Cave appears to be unhistoric, but I gather it is bottomless and stretches back to Loch Duntelchaig. Nothing remains of Brinmore kirk, but at Brinmore Farm is supposed to be an old burying ground sitting on even arable land, and never cropped or cultivated by man in living memory.

Tomintoul House is quite a mansion, and was built for the local doctor, but is now the Flichity estate office.

Before you reach East Croachy, a road to the west branches off to Dalcrombie, for centuries belonging to the MacGillivrays, offshoots of the Dunmaglass family. It is said that the last member of this worthy family hit a fellow on the head with a bottle, and left the district!

The village is East Croachy; the post office, Aberarder; and the Church is Brin! But they are all one!

Aberarder House was the seat of a cadet family of MacKintoshes for close on three centuries, and several of this distinguished family became Provosts of Inverness, particularly John MacKintosh about 1800, whose portrait by Raeburn hangs in the Town Hall, Inverness. The house was originally built in 1663 by the brothers, Lauchlan and Ewan MacKintosh of Moy Hall, and after his defeat at Culloden, Prince Charlie is said to have gone to Aberarder seeking refuge. A more recent proprietor was the late Major-General Beckwith-Smith, who commanded a British Division in Singapore, and died in a Japanese P.O.W. camp. In May, 1949, his widow sold the estate, comprising some 7,587 acres.

Duncan MacKintosh, the 15th son of Lauchlan Mor, 16th chief of the clan, was the first MacKintosh of Aberarder, and his son, William, ultimately became known as *A' Baillidh Dubh* — the Black Baillie. His name used to be seen on the door lintel in a chimney lintel of the old house. Another relic of the time also remains — a cairn of stones about a quarter of a mile west of the house, where criminals were hanged by Aberarder. A stump, attached to the Cairn, was supposed to have been part of the gallows.

According to tradition, the Black Baillie came into possession of the neighbouring property of Glenbeg by foul means. The proprietor of Glenbeg, it seems, was a very strong man, but with a passionate and hasty nature. And the story goes that the Black Baillie told a servant to take a sledge cart over to Glenbeg and help himself to some stooks of corn and bring them back to Aberarder. At first the servant hesitated, but his master assured him that no harm would befall him, and that he personally would stand between him and all danger. The fellow was persuaded to go, and when he was preparing his load, Glenbeg got word of what was going on in his fields, and seizing a club, rushed to the scene of the theft. In a fit of temper he killed the servant with a swing of his club.

When his rage subsided, Glenbeg was shocked by what he had done, and left the country immediately, never to return. So the Black Baillie stepped in, and thus the Glenbeg estate was added to Aberarder!

Until fairly recent times the keeping of a "wake" after death was in common vogue, and at one time in the Dunmaglass district a special form of wake, the *"tigh faire,"* was the practice of the people. The body was taken to a large barn, cleaned out for the occasion, then the country folk gathered round each evening before burial to keep the wake with music, songs, dancing and stories of the past.

3. FINE HOUSES

It seems incredibly absurd that some of the best farming land has been taken over for the expansion of housing estates; and that's the fate of the farm of Hilton, on the outskirts of Inverness.

I wonder what General Wade would have had to say about it all! He made the first road through this area, and more recently it became known as the Old Edinburgh Road. But it disappears into rough hillside on the southern edge of Strathnairn.

The name of Castleheather is comparatively recent, and has been derived from the less romantic "Castleleather" or "Castlelezar." I suppose the present name is more pleasant to the ear! However, Castleleather is taken from the Gaelic *caisteal* and *leitir* (so often anglicised as "letter"), and means a hillside or slope, though an alternative suggested derivation is "the slope with its back to the sun."

It was the seat of the Frasers of Castleleather, and one of this family, Major James Fraser, took his horse all the way to France, and brought home Simon, Lord Lovat, who was seeking refuge over there. Major Fraser of Castleleather was descended from a younger son of the laird of Culduthel, and died in the year 1760 at the ripe old age of 90. His life-size portrait hangs in Inverness Town House, and was painted about 1725.

Only part of the old house, as we know it today, existed at the time of Culloden, and was built from the actual stones of an old castle, the site of it being still visible a couple of hundred yards from the farm. A contractor by the name of MacDonald (who built the Inverness Suspension Bridge) was responsible for the additional building during his tenancy of the house, when it belonged to the late James Howe. The front doorstep is believed to be the largest slab of slate ever to come out of Caithness.

Between Castleheather and Druidtemple the two attractive residences of Glendruidh and Aird are comparatively modern. Aird House was presumably the coaching house of Glendruidh, but I can find little information about the other. It may have been a Dower House to Leys, and certainly it was originally only half its present size. The new section includes a tower, and a unique circular room, reputed to be haunted. There's a ghost too at Aird, but I have yet to find out what shape or form either of them take!

A forebear, Malcolm Fraser of Ruthven, believed to have been descended from the Frasers of Farraline, was in possession of

Culduthel in 1619. Both Culduthel and Castleleathers were part of the Castle lands of Inverness before that, and as such their superior was the Earl of Huntly. The Culduthel property was sold to the Baillies of Dochfour in 1844.

Like all similar laird's houses in the vicinity of Inverness, Culduthel House has been altered and redesigned a good deal in the last two centuries. The lock and key of the front door of the 18th century house is in the Inverness Museum, and this actual house was built on the site of an earlier building towards the close of that century, or very early in the next one.

The builder was Col. James Fraser of Culduthel (1756-1816), who served in the army for a number of years in the East Indies and America. He married a Sutherlandshire lady, Millicent MacKay, whose family emigrated to Ravenshead in Lancashire, where her father was one of the founders of the first plate glass factories in the United Kingdom. The cost of building Culduthel House was defrayed by the success of that venture.

4. ECHOES OF THE PAST

Invernessians talk of the Stratherrick Road as the one which leads along Drumashie Moor, and joins the main Stratherrick road from Dores to the north of Achnabat. It is not a particularly interesting stretch of land nowadays, with a few scattered farms, and plenty wide open spaces, but I will try and mention the few existing points of interest as we travel along it.

Leaving Inverness, we find two main approaches to this highway — by Drummond Road, or by breaking away from the Dores Road at the former Rosedene Nursing Home, almost opposite the favourite Ness Islands, a popular rendezvous for courting couples!

The white iron gates on our left, as we leave the town, guard the entrance to Lochardil House, a comparatively modern building, belonging to Ian MacDonald, the timber merchant. The house is of no historical significance, but at the end of the last century was the residence of the late Charles Fraser MacIntosh, the great historian and one-time M.P. for the Northern Counties.

Then a little way past Drumdevan, on the opposite side of the road, we find the Boar Stone, a broad, upright piece of sandstone sculptured with an ancient boar surmounted by two circles, one within the other, like a primitive target! The circles may signify the sun, but the boar, a wild beast of the chase, was the symbol of one of the Pictish tribes, whose seat of government was at Inverness. This carving, as an explanatory notice board nearby relates, is possibly two thousand years old and one of the most remarkable of its kind in Scotland.

On the moor, past Essich, is a long cairn, Glascharn, similar to the Clava cairns, which has evidently been a burial place. However, it is mostly broken up now and scattered, and many of the stones have been borrowed to build dykes; but there seems little doubt that in its perfect state it contained three burial chambers, one at each end, and another in the centre. The whole tumulus extended for some 120 yards.

The Drumashie Moor is bleak, and the few crofts on the roadside are grazed from other farms. Loch Ashie, itself, forms the main reservoir for Inverness, the water, as we have already seen, being pumped by pipeline to Oldtown of Leys reservoir two miles away.

Between Loch Ashie and Loch Duntelchaig is *Cathair Fhionn* or Fingal's Stone, where the famous Druid king is supposed to have watched the fray of one of his many murderous battles. Dotted about

Ashie Moor are various tumuli, which obviously tell of bygone strife, and one particular heap of stones is supposed to represent *Caisteal an Dunriachaidh* — the Castle of the King of the Sea — but little seems to be known of its significance.

It may have had something to do with the ghostly battle between ancient warriors, still reputed to be seen soon after dawn on a May morning. In 1870-71, the spectral fray was witnessed, and caused much excitement in the newspapers, as to whether it was a mirage of the fighting in France. The scenes have been very vivid — large bodies of men in close formation and smaller forces of cavalry facing an attacking army marching from the east; wounded men clapping spaghnum moss to their wounds and binding it on with strips torn from their shirts.

On one occasion a man cycling to Inverness saw three horsemen in front of him on the road. He followed for a distance, then, turning a corner, ran right into them, and to his amazement straight through them; falling off his bicycle in horror! I'm not surprised!

West from the cross roads, where the road verges into the Kindrummond road, you may be able to find an old well, called the Well of the Beard, so named because men drinking from it frequently dipped their beards in the water. One tale records that a bearded packman was murdered there, and that the spot is consequently haunted, giving rise to another possible name, the well of the Spectre!

5. ANCIENT LANDS

It was in the year 1732 that General Wade drew out the plans to start
work on his famous military road connecting the two army fortifications of Fort George and Fort Augustus, and the last time I motored
along a section of it I guessed that very little re-surfacing had been
done to it since Wade's time! However, today, part of it forms what
Invernessians call the Dores Road; Dores folk call it the Stratherrick
road; while further on it is merely the high road to Fort Augustus.

Only part of Wade's road follows its own course, between Dores
and Whitebridge, the rest verging into the more modern county road
made at a later date.

But let's start at the beginning, and call in at Holm Mills, one of
the foremost woollen mills in the Highlands, which has been
handling wool since its foundation away back about 1780.

It began as one of the smaller mills in the north, supplying carding
wool to the country community and preparing it for hand spinning.
Since the invention by Awkright of the spinning wheel, the whole
textile industry was revolutionised, and most of the spinning later was
done in the factories, so that instead of having his suit woven by the
woman of the house, the average farmer sent his wool along to the
mills, where it was woven with much less trouble. Thus a hundred
and one small mills sprung up all over the countryside, including
Holm Mills, and at Avoch, Kiltarlity, Tomatin and Skye, to mention
a few.

Historically, perhaps Borlum is the most outstanding farm in the
district, though I dare say the memories of the past and the famous
people who live there are long since forgotten.

About five hundred years ago it fell into the hands of a family of
MacKintoshes, remained so until the early 18th century, and being a
sept of the Clan Chattan, living in an outpost of the MacKintosh
country, they were compelled to be on the look out for invading
armies, and assist in their final expulsion if they should invade. As a
consequence of holding such a precarious position, they became
formidable and ferocious, the scourge of the district. Indeed, they
were a wild lot, dangerous even to their friends.

However, in later days, one member of the family became very
distinguished, Brigadier MacKintosh of Borlum, who commanded
the Highlanders at the Battle of Preston in 1715, and was taken
prisoner and died in prison.

Borlum Castle, as the seat of the family became known, was

situated a little way from the present farm house, and a later building was called Ness Castle before the present house of that name was built. Old Borlum Castle, an extremely strong building, reputed to be impregnable, was a suitable home for such ruffians.

Two of the fiercest representatives of that family, Lord and Lady Borlum, lived in the time of James V, and the story of the murder of the venerable Provost Junor of Inverness merely goes to show the callous nature of this breed. The tale is told in great length in rather an interesting little book, *Historical and Traditional Sketches of Highland Families and the Highlands,* by an Inverness centenarian of the last century, John MacLean. He relates:

"The Laird's lady on one occasion went to Inverness, where her visits would be most agreeably dispensed with; or, in other words, her absence would be considered good company by the terrified inhabitants. She was followed by two mischievous imps, as train bearers, or lady's henchmen. In the course of her perambulations through the town, she was seen by the worthy Provost in a position 'that mantled to his cheek the blush of shame,' and he was so shocked at her rude and indelicate demeanour that he took courage to reprove her, exclaiming: 'O, fie, fie, Lady Borlum'."

She was furious and struck dumb with rage. The author vividly describes how, raising herself to her full height, she slowly turned away her flaming eye, saying, "You shall dearly pay for this," and passed on.

Home she went to tell her husband, and together they planned revenge. Their two sons were assigned the deed, and when the provost made his usual evening stroll towards Campfield (now believed to be on the Essich road near the town boundaries) the sons set upon him, stabbed him to death, then hid his body under a bush, where it was later found.

Strong suspicions at once rested on the Borlum family, and after a day or two there seemed no doubt about the assassins, and as John MacLean writes:

"Meetings after meetings were held to bring them to punishment; but the town council, although eager enough to avenge the death of their chief magistrate, dreaded the ferocity and power of Borlum (who was a member of the council), the more particularly as he was backed by the friendship and power of the Earl of Huntly, at that time exercising almost regal authority in the north, and by whom, black MacKintosh of Borlum was always protected from the consequences of his evil deeds. The council, therefore, however reluctantly, were obliged to abandon the idea of punishing the assassins, and all they could do to show their respect for the deceased provost, and their detestation and horror of his murderers, was to pass a resolution that no member of the Borlum family should ever be eligible for a seat in the town council of Inverness — a resolution ever after adhered to."

In 1766 Borlum was purchased by a Mr Fraser, of the East India Company, a descendant of the House of Foyers.

Aldourie Castle, between the Dores Road and the River Ness, is no more a castle than Leys or Ness Castle, and is not an old building as a whole. One part, however, *does* date back to the 15th century. The main building was erected about the middle of last century by Sheriff William Fraser-Tytler, whose family have lived there till it was recently broken up into flats, and the kitchen wing was added just prior to the First World War.

In 1746 a son, Charles Grant, was born to a man of the Shewglie (Glenurquhart) family, Alex. Grant, who, due to his skill in battle, was better known as the Swordsman. At the time of his son's birth, Alexander was serving with the Jacobite army, and stationed in Inverness. The story is told that he and his companions hurried out to Aldourie to the christening of the young babe, called Charles, after the Prince, and crossed their broadswords over the baby's cradle during the christening ceremony.

The youthful Charles grew up to become Chairman of the East India Company, and was a great friend of Clive and Warren Hastings. For many years, too, he represented Inverness-shire in Parliament, and a fine portrait of him by Raeburn hangs in the Inverness County Buildings. His son, Charles, became Lord Glenelg; and another son, Robert, was later Sir Robert Grant, both medallists in mathematics at Cambridge.

I remember, as a boy, sailing up the whole stretch of the Caledonian Canal, from Fort William to Inverness, by MacBrayne's steamer. It was a pleasant trip, made mostly by tourists in the summer months, but, before the Canal was made, a regular steamer service ploughed back and forth along Loch Ness, calling at the various piers en route between Aldourie and Fort Augustus, sailing on a regular schedule for more than a hundred years. A succession of galleys, six in all, were built at Aldourie, though boat building has long since ceased here as in these early days. General Wade built a decked vessel, carrying about a dozen small guns, and I understand a couple of them are still preserved at Aldourie.

Talking of ships, one of the earliest visitors to Dores was Saint Columba, who landed in Dores Bay in skin coracles with twelve attendant monks, and from there proceeded over land to Inverness. However, there's quite a possibility he founded a Church on the site of the present one, as it is believed a Church stood on the same spot all through the centuries.

Dores is an attractive little place by the waters of Loch Ness, not only for summer visitors and retired residents, but also for the famous Loch Ness monster, which during an unrevealed life-time has made frequent appearances in this vicinity.

Dores was the birthplace of Captain John MacKay, one of the discoverers of Queensland, where the town of MacKay was built in his honour. He is described by a clansman who knew him as a short, square man with a pointed beard, and a native Gaelic speaker.

6. WADE'S ROAD

At Dores, General Wade's Road follows its own course along the edge of Loch Ness, through Inverfarigaig, to Foyers, and joins the main Fort Augustus thoroughfare at a point north of Whitebridge. It is the most direct route to Foyers, the one followed by the buses, but the least populated. By turning left in the centre of Dores village, up Kindrummond Brae, we would presently find ourselves mid heather-clad hills and heading straight into Stratherrick, a new world of kindly folk and hospitality.

It is difficult to determine the best road to take on an exploring expedition of this kind; we can easily go round in circles, and can find so many side attractions to take us off the beaten track. However, let's make a start and climb Kindrummond and return to Dores for the loch road in a later chapter.

In a dip in the road, before the ascent to Balnafoich, is a well, where, as local tradition relates, a mother and son perished in the great storm of 1826, and the boy was found with a piece of sugar candy still in his mouth. For many years this storm was remembered, and afterwards all events as births, marriages and deaths, were referred to by the people as having taken place before or after the year of the storm. It is recorded that two neighbouring sheep farmers lost 1300 and 1100 sheep respectively that night of havoc. The summer and autumn before had been very dry, and corn crop so short that it could not be cut, and had to be pulled out by the roots. Balnafoich was formerly a shooting lodge.

Beside Wester Erchite steading are the ruins (now only rubble, almost overgrown) of Erchite Castle, which was destroyed after the '45. However, history recalls that at this time Erchite belonged to a Captain John Fraser, a staunch supporter of the Prince, who headed a party of his clan, ten days before Culloden, and marched to Culloden Castle to capture President Forbes, a supporter of the Government. But on approaching the house they were spotted by a sentinel on the turrets, who gave the alarm, and the attackers were met with "a fearful discharge of shot, which wounded many, but killed none," as one historian relates.

Presently we come to the junction of the Drumashie road, and then find Achnabat standing alone on a slight promontory, over-looking the sombre waters of Loch Duntelchaig, with the Pike Loch in the foreground.

An inn once stood at Achnabat, though I have yet to decide on its true situation. Duncan believes its position was about 500 yards south-west of the farm, because he took cartloads of stones from this supposed site. Somebody else suggested it formed part of the original steading; while a third suggestion is that it stood across the road from the farm buildings. Tradition tells us that it was a favourite haunt of drovers, reivers, smugglers and travellers; and, as free fights were rife on the green beside it, we find the derivation of the name as "the field of the sticks."

Funeral parties have been known to have spent days there, the coffin being left half forgotten at the Inn!

The drive towards Torness takes you along the edge of Loch Cé-Glais; and the story is told about a man making his way to Communion, being overtaken by mist, and seeing a vision of the Devil driving a coach and four up the loch!

On the hill of Tom na Croich, Lord Lovat (of an early date) hanged offenders from a steep rock in the days of heritable jurisdiction. The Lovats stayed at *Croit nan Cearc* (the hen's hillock), situated on a terrace on a small ridge about 600 yards east of Torness Bridge, before coming to the Aird district in the 12th century.

The small estate of Dunchea was owned by a Fraser, and purchased by the Farraline Estates on his death about a century ago. Part of the steading and two workmen's houses are still there, but almost derelict now, and the lands worked along with Abersky. Dunchea was once noted for its cream, the pastures being so good that the cows produced rich milk.

A house built into the hillside to the south of Abersky is an ice-house, with a flagstone floor. I believe they were quite common in by-gone days and were equivalent to our modern refrigerators.

Turning right at Torness Bridge, we may take the road to Leadclune, another small estate at one time belonged to a Fraser family. In fact, it can be said that the whole of Stratherrick used to be owned by various families of Frasers, individual branches, though very often related by marriage.

The old house of Leadclune, built in 1760, is now a charming farm house. It still reveals traces of former days. For instance, some of the window panes in the drawing-room have been well preserved, being thick and not so transparent as the glass in everyday use now. A small recess in the kitchen wall brings back memories of home-made bread; but the cellar, alas! has been sealed up!

The inner partition walls of some of the rooms are particularly ancient, dating back some 250 years; and until then masons used a mixture of cow dung and lime as a plaster. The house is a rambling one, with three storeys.

Long ago, I'm told, farm workers on Leadclune were punished for their mistakes by being sent away out to the peat beds to cut peat on wet days, and the late Dan Shaw, Croftdhu, loved to tell the tale of two workers, who, on reaching the peat beds, stuck their long spades into the ground, hung their jackets on them, and made for home, where they spent the rest of the day toasting their toes at the bothy fire. Then, in the late afternoon, they returned for their jackets, now soaked with rain, and came back to the farm wearing their drenched apparel.

On seeing this pathetic sight, the farmer, a member of the Frazer (spelt with a "z") family took pity on them, and in spite of their penance brought them into his house, and gave them each a good strong dram!

From Errogie manse I looked across Loch Mhor to the lovely stone house of Farraline which hides many secrets and lore within its aging walls, and those in the village of Errogie, who remember the last of the Frasers of Farraline, tell me they were much revered and loved by the people in Stratherrick in their day; and their name is still cherished by all who knew them.

Until about 60 years ago, Loch Mhor was made up of two separate lochs — Loch Farraline and Loch Garth — joined by a narrow canal; and when plans were drawn up to build an aluminium factory at Foyers, it was decided to join the two lochs, and raise the level of Loch Garth, by a dam, thus forming a united reservoir. Consequently, much of the area on the loch's sides was submerged, and the road on the Farraline side raised to a higher level.

About a hundred yards along from the manse stands "The Ark," opposite the Free Church; and I'm told it was originally built for the schoolmaster for the sum of £70! Prior to the Education Act of 1872, the schoolmaster was dominie of a small church, now submerged, and was succeeded by a Government teacher. The name of the house is an unusual one, but owes its origin to the fact that when the loch level rises, it is liable to become swamped with the synthetic tide.

Errogie Post Office was an old inn until about 50 years ago, and the proprietor sold more whisky in it than any of the other inns in the district put together! An old hosteller, Callum MacInnes, a real worthy, who could neither read nor write, was the best card player in all Stratherrick! Full of wonderful stories, his imagination being more vivid than his actual recollections, he often liked to crack with the lads about the times he spent in distant waters, though I doubt he never travelled further than his native Skye.

"Tell us what it was like in Australia," the lads in the village would coax him.

"Ach, I never landed there. I only sighted it," was his usual hedging reply.

Both Aultnagoire and Aultmhor are on the Inverfarigaig road, and I stopped my car in Inverfarigaig Pass, beneath the mighty shadow of Dundeardil, to look at a roadside monument erected in memory of a distinguished geologist, James Bryce, who was killed while in pursuit of his favourite science in July, 1877.

The Forestry Commission have taken over much of the land in the Inverfarigaig district, and I think the lovely trees in the Pass are some of the finest I have ever seen, planted about 1890, when a scheme was devised to plant ornamental trees from Inverfarigaig to Foyers, but almost as soon as it was started, the idea was abandoned.

Hidden in the hillside near Dirichurachan is a cave, supposed to be haunted by an old man, whose crying and wailing foretell imminent death in the district!

At Balchuirn (town of the cairn) are the ruins of an old castle, and nearby, overlooking the Farigaig, was the chapel and graveyard of St Moluag, a noted saint of the Church of Iona, who died in 592, five years before St Columba. We can only discern a few stones and bushes where the chapel and yard were supposed to be. A former school stood at Balchuirn before the present one was built at Bunchruben.

For some time Bochruben formed part of a barony possessed by a family of Ogilvies, afterwards acquired by the Earl of Huntly, who disposed of it to The MacIntosh; and later it became the property of Fraser of Balnain in the last half of the 18th century.

The whole country between Bochruben and Ballaggan is called Baile Cheatharnaich, and its fertile slopes were once thickly popu-lated by some of the most notorious thieves in the country.

7. MURDER — AND MYSTERY

Just below the former policeman's house at Dores, one of the last cottages on the west end of the village, there used to be an old stone, *Clach nam Meirlach* (the stone of the thieves), now under water, but significant in being used as a tide mark by raiding parties, where they could reckon the height of the water at Bona Ford, a popular crossing place to the other side of the River Ness.

Leaving the village, the first place we come to on the roadside is a small croft, Balachladaich, which has changed hands several times in recent years; and a few hundred yards along the road from it, the Witch's Bridge is so called because witches often were seen sitting on its parapet walls. The suspicion of ruins nearby seems to suggest that the witch inhabited a croft as well! But the latter (if not the former, too), may easily be hearsay, as at one time the whole road to Foyers was "alive" with cottages and crofts.

A little way past Whitefield Gate Cottage, now only a summer residence and otherwise deserted, we come upon a small piece of arable land, once the site of an old change house, visited by Dr Johnson and Boswell in 1773. The house was called *An Ithur Mhor,* and there's rather an interesting story connected with it.

At the time of Culloden the inn-keeper was an old lady, who lived with her beautiful grand-daughter. One day an officer of Cumberland's army entered the inn seeking refreshment, and, seeing the fair maid, tried to assault her. But the grandmother intervened, and the girl made her escape, fleeing over the hill to the neighbouring district of Baile Cheatharnaich (that's the area between Bochruben and Ballaggan) to fetch help from some of the lads.

They returned to the change house with her, only to find the grandmother lying dead in the chair, choked by the officer in his anger. On hearing about the incident, Duke William was furious, and the officer was severely punished and made to pay blood money.

Another tale tells of a paymaster of the Fort Augustus forces, on his way back from Inverness with the soldier's pay, resting here for the night, and being found dead in the morning, robbed of his money, and no trace remaining of either horse or harness ever after!

The point where Inverfarigaig comes into view is the scene of another spicy little murder, near to a spot notorious for its nest of robbers. Not long after Culloden, a shoemaker's wife from Fort Augustus, who sold groceries and travelled about in her small cart, pulled by a piebald pony, was robbed and killed, and it was supposed that the occupants of the two nearby houses and the people from Cheatharaich had done the deed. Anyway, some time later, several folk were seen in a local sermon house wearing vests made from the old woman's cloak. Her body was never found, but the pony, making its way home, wandered to *Dail Bhreac,* where the old laird of Foyers, Bonaid Odhair, was living in concealment in a cave at the time. He ordered the pony's feet to be tied together and had it thrown into Lochan Torr an tuill.

Many well-known families of Frasers of Stratherrick lie buried in the parish kirkyard of Boleskine, and, although I have not yet been able to find it, I believe there is a tombstone in the south wall on the grave of Donald Fraser of Erchite, bearing the marks of bullets on it. The story in this case is also post-Culloden, and tells of a funeral party being split up by the mischievous action of one of the mourners At the time, a cart carrying military provisions passed by on its way to Fort Augustus; and one of the mourners pinched a loaf of bread off the cart and threw it to some dogs. He was immediately arrested and marched off to the Fort; but, before leaving, the soldiers fired a volley of shots indiscriminately into the funeral party, and only succeeded in hitting the tombstone.

Next morning, the minister of Boleskine, a staunch supporter of the Government, followed his parishioner to Fort Augustus, where he met the Duke and succeeded in obtaining the fellow's release.

A little building in the churchyard is a watchtower (I came across a similar one at Dunlichity), where relatives guarded new graves against body-snatchers.

An old Church also once stood in the churchyard, and the present Boleskine House was formerly the manse. However, by an arrangement with the Frasers of Lovat, Church and manse were transported to Drumtemple, near Lochbranside, and Boleskine House was built by Lovat on the hillside, overlooking the churchyard.

The folk of the district still remember with a mixture of horror and amusement the antics of a former proprietor, Aleister Crowley (or, as he called himself, Lord Boleskine), who was one of the greatest practical jokers ever known in these parts. He had spent years abroad, and owned a wonderful collection of skins and weapons, and would often "scare the daylights" out of the community by appearing fantastically garbed on the open highway, accompanied by servants similarly clad. Many are the stories told about him, and some say he practised a form of black magic in one of the rooms set aside as "The Temple."

So we come to Foyers, the village which has sprung up in 60 years from a small estate by the introduction of the British Aluminium

Company factory on Loch Ness side.

When the Company bought the estate in 1895 only the burnt-out ruins of Foyers House remained standing, and it was presently re-roofed with corrugated iron, and used as an hostel. But it was later pulled down, and a modern terrace built on its site. Yew trees were planted beside it at the time of Culloden, and, when the estate was sold, they were protected by a fence, now long since disappeared. But the trees are still there.

For seven years Hugh Fraser of Foyers took refuge in the hills after Culloden, and, although the Redcoats hunted him day and night, his cave of concealment was never divulged. The local people nicknamed him Bonaid Odhair—Dun-bonnet—and could openly talk of him, while the soldiers never discovered his true identity.

The cave appears to have been well hidden in a district known as the Camus, and near it, I am told, is a yew tree, from which the Frasers took wood for their bows and arrows in earlier days. One story tells of a girl bringing food to the fugitive, being followed by a soldier guessing her errand. But the old laird spotted the man long before he reached the retreat, shot him dead in his tracks, and later buried him where he fell.

Another day a boy, carrying a cask of beer, was met by a party of Government soldiers on a brae near the Falls of Foyers, and questioned on the whereabouts of his master. But the stout lad refused to divulge the secret, even though the soldiers slashed off one of his hands. The cask tumbled off the lad's shoulders and into the chasm below, since known as the Cask's Leap.

The Falls of Foyers have for long been a favourite attraction to the tourists. Even Rabbie Burns, on a visit to the Highlands, came to see them and mentions them in one of his poems.

8.   THE FORTY-FIVE

Many are the beds and caves where Prince Charlie is reputed to have slept after Culloden, and it is difficult to verify their authenticity. However, we do know that after the battle he retreated on horseback through Strathnairn towards Gorthleçk.

The story is told of a little girl of the house of Gortuleg, looking out of an upstairs window and sighting the approach of the horsemen. Downstairs, in his armchair, sat the 80-year-old Lovat (who was staying with the child's father), while the ladies of the house, both staunch Jacobites, prepared a meal intended to be a victory feast. But their hopes were soon dashed when the wounded Highlanders arrived, and they were presently tearing apart their garments of lace to bind up the wounds of the conquered.

There was only time for a hasty meal, before the fugitives had to set off towards Fort Augustus and the road to the west; and tradition relates that, while eating in an upstairs room, the Prince was disturbed by approaching Redcoats, and had to make his escape from a back window. Meanwhile, the Redcoats were hammering at the front door, strongly barred from the inside, and, incidentally, the old bar can still be seen in its original position fitting into the wall, in use yet in what is now Gorthleck farm house.

The upstairs room is a charming one, and you can well imagine the Prince's hazardous escape from the window's height to the ground. The apartment is known yet as Prince Charlie's room.

Gorthleck House, nearby, may have been standing at the '45, but it was very much smaller then.

We cross the waters of Loch Mhor to reach Aberchalder, Ballindalloch and Migovie, and the road to the latter is both bad and bumpy, skirting the often dried-up Migovie Bay.

At one time Migovie was a sheep farm, let with Aberchalder, and all vestiges of fences were removed to allow free scope for the sheep. Then along came John Fraser in 1935, with other ideas of farming; and to-day fences are still going up, and the land gradually being brought back into cultivation.

A little way off the Migovie road you will find rather an attractive old bridge, carrying a disused road leading to Aberchalder Meal Mill. But the mill has been derelict for 25 years, when the last miller, Hugh Fraser, died.

An old drove road, believed to be the one mentioned in D. K. Broster's "The Flight of the Heron," passes beside Easter Aber-

DULSIE BRIDGE

CAWDOR PARISH CHURCH

THE BOAR STONE

Photo: Andrew Paterson

THE AUTHOR AT CULLODEN CAIRN

chalder, and, if follówed, I am told, would take the traveller through the hills into the Kingussie district, a distance of some twelve miles. By normal road passage the journey to Kingussie is about 60 miles.

The Deserter's Cave on the hill, *Leachd-nan-Cisteachan*, beyond Garthbeg, was the hide-out of a fugitive from the 79th Camerons about 130 years ago; and it was said that even the keenest and most experienced scout would have difficulty in finding its position. Actually, the entrance is so small that a man has to bend double to crawl inside and be content when there to remain in a sitting position.

Not unnaturally, the deserter, one of the Clan Fraser, soon became weary of his precarious existence, and applied to Fraser of Foyers to approach the authorities regarding his pardon; but without success. So he next turned to the parish minister, another clansman, a chaplain to the forces, and presently the erstwhile deserter was now once again rehabilitated to the incomparable 79th.

Boleskine Church, built in 1777, is the highest building in altitude in Stratherrick — 800 feet above sea level.

At least traces of gold have been found in minute quantities in the river bed of the Fechlin at Glenlia, where the water enters the tunnel leading to the aluminium factory at Foyers. Traces of gold have been brought up from the bottom of Loch Ness, at the time of a depth survey of some of our Highland lochs, 50 years ago.

We find a splendid example of a Wade's bridge on approaching Whitebridge, a typical humpy-back type, though unused since 1938, when a new one was erected to carry the main road. During the last war the Newfoundlanders, who were employed cutting trees in Dell Wood, were camped near the bridge.

Further on we come to Wester Drummond and the road end to Knockie on our right, and it is quite a considerable distance from the "broad highway" to Knockie Lodge, beautifully situated between two lochs, Loch nan Lann and Loch Knockie. Rather a far-fetched story is told about a lady, dressed in a crinoline, being swept by a gust of wind from the heights of the Suidhe to Loch nan Lann, a distance of about a mile; and she was never quite the same afterwards!

Knockie was once the seat of the Frasers of Lovat, and the design of the original building (to which have been added wings on either side) is similar to that of Gorthleck. One of the old Frasers of Knockie, Captain Simon Fraser, compiled an interesting collection of Highland melodies.

At the time of Culloden there lived in Fort Augustus a man by the name of Corrie or Gorrie, who had heard of the great atrocities and the defeat of the battle, and decided to take upon himself the job of ridding the country of that English butcher, the Duke of Cumberland. So he took up position at a point of the road near Glendoebeag, where he hoped to ambush the Duke. But when the troopers arrived he lost his nerve and bolted down the Glendoe burn to seek refuge in a cave on Loch Ness side, to this day known as Corrie's cave.

Another tale concerns a bunch of Lochaber reivers, who went in search of cattle down Speyside, from where they drove off a herd, and brought them home through Stratherrick. At Glendoebeag, the Strathdearn men, under the leadership of Iain Beag McAnndra, a famous archer, caught up with the reivers, and ambushed them at the ford over Glendoe burn. One of the raiders, Mac 'ille Mhiorran, was killed, and is buried under a flat stone somewhere in the vicinity. The others fled, leaving the cattle to their rightful owners.

Yet another interesting anecdote reminds us of the Irish famine of the mid-19th century, when two boats struck anchor at the mouth of the Glendoe burn, and took on board loads of farm produce to relieve the serious food position on the Emerald Isle.

So we come to Fort Augustus at the head of Loch Ness, recognised as perhaps the most central spot in the Highlands of Scotland.

9. HALLOWED CLOISTERS

It is not often that I lunch in silence; but then, it's not every day that I'm guest of the Abbot and the Monks at St. Benedict's Abbey, Fort Augustus.

"It's part of monastic life to be recollected, and this is greatly helped by silence at proper times and places," explains one of the brethren," particularly so in the Chapter House, Refectory, Library and Cloisters. Duty and charity naturally excuse us from this law of silence, such as looking after guests, serving at meals and educational work."

Perhaps it seemed strange to me, not of their Faith, to find myself seated in the centre of the great hall, while the monks took up their accustomed seats around the panelled walls of the refectory. Yet, I was honoured to be among them.

As we sat in silence amidst the clatter of dishes, a monk sat in his pedestal, a wooden pulpit mounted on the wall at one end of the refectory, and read passages from the Bible and a chapter from a modern classic. My ears were unaccustomed to this practice, and I could only pick up an occasional sentence, though, I was later told, the monks scarcely miss a word.

The meal finished, the monks rose and the Abbot gave thanks in Latin; then, donning their black hoods, the brethren fell into double file, and processed out of the refectory and along the cloisters to the Church for thanksgiving, chanting one of the psalms. It was an impressive sight, and one we do not often see.

Perhaps, before describing the Abbey, it would be wise to deal for a moment with the history behind it, as the Benedictine Fathers have only been in residence for the last 75 years. Prior to 1876, it belonged to the Frasers of Lovat, and was originally built as a fort by Marshall Wade in 1729, to help quell disturbances among the warlike Highlanders. However, thirteen years previously a barrack was built (now the site of the Lovat Arms Hotel), but was later considered insufficient.

The old name of Fort Augustus was Kilchuimein, but when the fort was built, Wade re-named it, after William Augustus, Duke of Cumberland, the youngest son of George II; and gradually the former place-name fell into disuse.

In 1876 the transformation of the buildings commenced, and two of the bastions, at the extremities of the south wing, were completely removed. The building, standing between them, known as the

"Duke's House," was also pulled down; and in other wings some of the old thick walls were retained as foundations of the new. The alterations took four years to complete, and in 1880 the Benedictine Monks began at Fort Augustus a life of Prayer and Work.

As we enter the hospice at the main door, we see an accurate model of the old fort, made by one of the brethren during the First War from original drawings in the War Office. Two beautifully carved early 18th century chairs on either side were gifted by an old Catholic family of Jerninghams, and came from Costessie Hall, Norfolk. However, this portion of the hospice never formed part of the fort, as the low round arch leading into the main building was the chief entrance from the drawbridge.

On either side of the hospice passage, into which we enter through the arch, are guest rooms, formerly vaulted guardrooms. One of these is now a shop used for the sale of souvenirs and pamphlets to visitors, and opposite, on the site of the old fort prison, the monks have built the Chapel of Holy Relics, decorated with mural paintings after the style of the Roman Catacombs. The stone altar was designed and made in the Abbey, and the Cross decorated with an assortment of many Scottish stones. The original brick floor, dating back to about the time of Culloden, was made from local clay, quite probably from Inchnacardoch.

On the second floor of the hospice, the former fort armoury has been converted into reception rooms for distinguished visitors; and it is interesting to find the Latin word "Pax"—meaning "peace"— inscribed on the fireplace beneath a statue of St Benedict, in the very room where Cumberland's soldiers kept their weapons of war.

Since the beginning of the century the monks have been erecting their Church. The lofty central part with a temporary nave and sanctuary was put up in the First War, and in 1949 work started again, after an interval, on a permanent nave to harmonise with the part already there.

The giant organ is almost the largest in Scotland, with more than 4,000 pipes, and in 1875 was the biggest private organ in existence. It has four keyboards and a hundred stops, and was originally built by Bryceson for a Mr Holmes, for his house in Regent's Park, but was removed to the old Albert Palace in Battersea Park in 1884. When the Palace was demolished ten years later, the organ was purchased by the Abbey, and transported there by rail and steamer, and stowed away for another twenty years in the largest room in the monastery.

Adjoining the Church I was shown into the blessed Sacramental Chapel, in which the canopy over the altar was presented to the Abbey by the Frasers of Lovat, in memory of the present Lord

Lovat's uncle, Major Hugh Fraser. Of unusual material and design, it is made of elaborately painted deerskin.

The Library is exceptionally fine with a collection of some 40,000 books, including very old original manuscripts. Perhaps the most remarkable of these is an autograph 11th century MS. of St Marianus Scotus, founder of the Abbey of Ratisbon or the "Monastery of St James of the Scots," to give its formal title. On the library walls hang portraits of cardinals connected with Scotland: Erskine, Beaton and Henry, Duke of York.

The old fort's Governor's House is now the sacristy, where I saw the most beautiful vestments used in the Church ceremonies; and the principal vesting table made from carved Spanish oak was also gifted to the Abbey by Lord Lovat.

The Cloisters connecting the quadrangular structure of the Abbey are paved with warm tinted tiles and lit by Gothic windows set in embrasures of the stone wall.

The northern side of the quadrangle is occupied by the Abbey School (founded in 1878), and its crowning feature is surely the tower, a hundred feet high, containing the great clock and carillon of nine bells. The School was intended to accommodate about seventy pupils, but I believe the scholars exceed that number, such is the standard of teaching in the classrooms. The Fathers of St Benedict devote much of their time to learning, and help in the teaching of the Classics.

The playgrounds are extensive with tennis courts, cricket fields and open-air swimming baths, and the school enjoys a growing reputation for proficiency, both in study and sport.

10.   HIGHLAND WATERWAY

Possibly the greatest engineering feat in the early 19th century was the building of the Caledonian Canal connecting east and west Scotland, and sparing many a hazardous passage around the Pentland Firth. A writer of the time estimated its cost as £300,000, with an annual revenue of £40,000, but considering the vast amounts paid in construction of modern hydro-electric schemes and similar transactions, I don't really think the cost was unreasonable. However, it has been in constant use ever since it was officially opened on an autumn day in 1822.

Can you imagine the scene, when a little steamer, the "Stirling Castle," left Muirtown Wharf, decorated from bow to stern with bunting, and carrying on board some of the very important members of the Canal Commission, other distinguished guests and a pipe band? Proudest of all that day must have been Thomas Telford, born a humble shepherd's son, but whose genius planned and laid out the whole construction of this wonderful waterway.

Thomas Telford will long be remembered as a pioneer in Scottish life, and the designer of over 1200 bridges, including the Dean Bridge in Edinburgh; and the Broomielaw in Glasgow. He also planned the Ellesmore Canal and was responsible for the making of over a thousand miles of roadway in the Highlands, Lanarkshire and Dumfries-shire.

Inverness is proud of its share in the Caledonian Canal, even though this waterway only skirts its boundaries; and the town has honoured the great engineer by naming a street and a road after him. The entry into the canal juts into the estuary of the Beauly Firth, and it is interesting and perhaps surprising to note that within the first half mile of canal we come to a little patch of land on the embankment where one could easily find a shamrock growing—for this is Irish soil! Formerly, it was a bog, but was filled up with soil brought over from Ireland by cargo vessels to act as ballast, when they sailed up the canal for their loads of potatoes. The G.P.O. telephone department now use this piece of ground as a telegraph pole dump, about a hundred yards from Muirtown Canal Swing Bridge.

Old Muirtown House is undated, but I believe a house has been on the site for centuries, and part of the present building might be from the original. At one time it was owned by a family of Cheviz, then Duffs, who succeeded in mortgaging the greater part of the property.

At the back of Craig Dunain hospital we find Craig Phadrig, a vitrified fort, believed to have been the stronghold of King Brude, though some say it dates back further than his time. It is now in fairly good preservation, and the outline of the foundation is easily distinguishable. One theory is that its position was chosen as a suitable height (555 feet), to communicate with other similar forts. Oblong in shape, it has both an outer and inner wall, with a natural entrance at the west end. A well at the east end is described as being "a natural reservoir."

Torvean ridge rather commends itself as being a suitable spot for a royal residence, and it has been suggested that the ridge was used as such and fortified with earthworks; that on the slope above stretched the huts of the community, and Craig Phadrig was used as a retreat for the people when faced with the enemy. The name of Torvean appears to mean "the hill of Bean"—he being a cousin of St Columba, whom he succeeded in the Abbacy of Iona.

The derivation of Tomnahurich is controversial. It may mean the hill of the boat, or the boat-shaped hill (as indeed it is), though another explanation is the Fairy Hill.

"Strange as it may seem to you this day," prophesied the Brahan Seer, "the time will come—it is not far off— when full-rigged ships will be seen sailing eastward and westward by Muirtown and Tomnahurich, near Inverness."

The great Coinneach Odhar was right again! The Caledonian Canal is the obvious answer.

The prophet then added,"that the day would come when Tomnahurich; or, as he called it *Tom nan Sithichean,* or "Fairy Hill," would be under lock and key, and the fairies secured within. As Tomnahurich is now a beautiful cemetery, it may be possible that the seer was referring to the dead bodies entombed therein.

Until living memory, Dochgarroch House was the family seat of a branch of the Clan MacLean; and a member of this family, John MacLean, seems to have spent most of his life as an outlaw. His troubles started when he returned home from Killiecrankie. For his part in the fray he was outlawed and took refuge in Strathglass until the amnesty of 1693, when all who showed title deeds and took oath of allegiance to King William were pardoned.

However, John MacLean went out again in the 1715 Rebellion, and consequently was outlawed again, and his mother and brother installed in his place. Again, he was pardoned, and at this time he built the House of Dochnalairg, where he lived undisturbed and surrounded by his followers.

Unfortunately, a number of Hessian soldiers came into the neighbourhood for a foraging party, and began to help themselves.

Whereupon, MacLean, with a handful of men, challenged them with sticks, actually killing one of the soldiers. For a third time the luckless laird sought refuge in the hills!

In 1740 he was persuaded to give himself up, and, as no one would bear witness that he was responsible for the killing of the soldier, he was liberated, and lived in peace for a few years, presently taking up residence in another house, near the scene of the scuffle, consequently called Battlefield.

11 SMUGGLERS

The Caiplich-Abriachan road branches off the main road to the west, and, though the upward climb is fairly acute, we are rewarded with a fine view to our left looking right down Loch Ness.

This district is ideal for home distilling of whisky! It's quiet and lonely, away from the population and outside interference, and I am sure this is how some old worthies of the past must have looked at life. Some of them had little else to do to earn a living. So several of them reverted to smuggling, and in spite of the gaugers, succeeded in disposing of large quantities of their own brew.

In quite recent times the best known smuggler in Caiplich was known as the "Swapper," a name pinned on him, due to his dealing ability, and his tendency for swapping goods instead of payment. During the First War he repeatedly distilled his own whisky in a little stone house about a mile from Ballimore, but his home at Caiplich is no longer in existence, and a lonely tree merely marks its site.

Nearer Abriachan, another smuggler, Duncan Fraser, became known as the King of Smugglers, and one of his bothies, on the ridge of *Carn an Leitre,* is still there.

The gaugers were ever after him, but never got him, and I believe he finally dumped all his gear—pot and worm—into Loch Laide, when some of the gaugers were hot on his trail; and they are still in the loch to-day. On one occasion, Duncan hung his cask of whisky on a hook in the hall of his house, hidden under a number of coats, and when the gaugers came round to search the house they failed to find it. then again he got his old mother to hide the cask up her skirt, while on a third instance he disguised his father as a corpse, laid out on the best room table, covered with a sheet, and tightly grasping the cask.

Beside one of the small crofts of Altourie is the tumble-down ruin of Wester Altourie, where a beautiful lady was murdered by her jealous husband, when he returned home to find her in the arms of another man. Before she died, the story goes, she managed to crawl for help to the neighbouring house, and some later tenants used to claim that they heard her knocking at the door in the middle of the night!

"We never heard anything unusual," I was told, "but I remember once seeing a strange light hovering in a hollow nearby. It seemed to rise in the air to a height of four feet, then suddenly faded out. I never discovered what it was!''

Part of this road forms a portion of the old hill road from Inverness, and further on it disappears into the waste boggy marshes. However, I believe it is along this way that the Thirteen Women of Glenurquhart set off in search of their husbands after the Battle of Culloden, hoping to find them in hiding and help heal their wounds.

I didn't expect to find a poet, author, and University graduate in these parts, but a peaceful life seems to appeal to Mrs Katharine Stewart an Edinburgh lady. A year ago she published her first book of poems, "Days of Grace," by Jeanne Dark, which is a delightful little collection of her lyrics. She graduated in foreign languages, and for a time stayed in France, teaching English in a French girls' school.

The community of Abriachan has greatly changed in the last twenty years, and at one time it was a thriving crofting area. Very few remain, the houses vacant, and the crofts' acreages worked as a single unit. Even the school, which once housed over a hundred pupils, is reduced to a mere two dozen.

Near the school the village hall was erected by the folk of Abriachan with their own hands and paid for out of local funds.

In past days feuds were quite common among the different sections of the community, one lot not being on speaking terms with another for long periods. I'm afraid we still find this failing among individuals everywhere to-day. Many of the population are incomers, and I note several of the old cottages have been modernised and turned into very comfortable homes, and favourite summer resorts for Invernessians.

If you take a stroll down to the shore at Brackla you may see The Black Rock, placed there in rather an unusual manner, according to tradition.

The story is about two witches from Dores (across the water) and Abriachan, who had a row with one another and started hurling great boulders across the loch. The rock from Dores fell short of its mark, landing in the water, and so it is believed that it lies yet on the water's edge near Brackla!

12.   THE KING'S DAUGHTER

John Cobb came to Temple Pier on Loch Ness in 1952 to attempt a new world speed record in his jet-propelled *"Crusader,"* and his tragic death, one still morning in September, brought sorrow to those folk in Glenurquhart, who had grown to know him like a personal friend; for John Cobb was a real gentleman, kindly, and respected by everyone he met.

Several attempts at trials were made, but from somewhere a breeze always seemed to spring up, until on this fatal September morning, conditions seemed ideal. The loch was calm as a mill-pond, and the accompanying boats were ordered to their action stations. But I have heard it said that the whole operation was organised in too much of a hurry, so that the wash from the vessels had not time to settle, before the *"Crusader"* began its run towards "The Measured Mile." Anyway, as it sped along the loch, eye-witnesses reported that it seemed to strike two or three waves, and the next moment it exploded and shattered into a thousand pieces. John Cobb's body was presently retrieved from the chill waters, and the *"Crusader"* found its last resting place in the alluvial bottom of Loch Ness.

The last boats on a regular steamer service called at Temple Pier just before the war, and, like many other Loch Ness piers, it has fallen into dereliction.

Of course, there was an old Druid Temple at Temple Pier—we are apt sometimes to forget derivations. A large rock marks the supposed site on the north side of the road, and nearby, also on the roadside, is St. Ninian's Well, believed to have been used in Druid times as a source of water. When workmen were building the new Loch Ness road they unearthed several interesting old coins at the well.

It appears that St Ninian came to that district, north and east of the Grampians, at the end of the fourth century to preach Christianity, but it is not quite certain whether he had direct contact with the Northern Picts. It is more probable that "the message of salvation" was first delivered by St Columba.

The building beside the site of the old temple, known as Temple House, is dated 1851, and the lady living in the east wing tells me that it was originally built as an inn, being close to the pier; but it was split up into individual houses for economical reasons.

Within the bounds of Tychat, according to legend, a stone on the loch shore was a favourite meeting place of witches. They would often be seen by the Glen folk in conference, under the presidency of the devil, who sat on a ledge of the rock, and played to them on his pipes (when not otherwise engaged in more serious business). The effect of the music was terrific and they indulged in pranks and cantrips, which the lithest athletes could not touch!

The rocky hill behind the crofts of Tychat and St Ninian's, known as Creag Ney, until the last war was thickly wooded, but, during that war, Canadian soldiers, billeted at Lochend, cut all the trees down and conveyed them to a sawmill near their billets.

Drumnadrochit Hotel, a large, comfortable establishment, was opened as an Inn before 1763, and in that year was under lease to James Grant of Shewglie. From 1779 it continued to prosper as a change-house.

A story is told of two brothers who heard of a wild boar's "nest" of "coolins" (or piglets) in a cave somewhere on the hillside at the back of the Hotel, and decided to explore the cave when the sow was not at home. On reaching the cave, one of the brothers, Donald, entered to get a "coolin" or two from the litter, while his brother, John, stayed outside on the look-out for the sow.

Suddenly a shadow flashed passed him, and in the nick of time John recognised the shape of the sow and managed to grab its tail. The entrance to the cave appears to be narrow, because its form, held tightly by the tail, completely blocked it, throwing the cave practically into total darkness.

"Man, what's blocking the light?" called out Donald from within.

"If this tail breaks," replied his breathless brother, "you'll soon find out what's blocking the light!"

The name Lewiston is the English name given to a village founded by Sir James Grant, with a view to keeping the local folk in the Glen and to stop emigration; and now it is a bonnie, little hamlet stretching on either side of the main road, along the banks of the River Coiltie. Borlum Bridge, across the river, is actually the third to be built over it, and from the front of the old smithy you can see the original piling alongside the present bridge. A spate in the river accounted for its downfall, when a large trunk washed down in the floods struck it, and carried it away with the loss of three lives.

The derivation of the "Coltie" is "the place of woods," and long ago forestry workers felled a quantity of birch trees nearer its source, using the spates to carry the logs down towards Loch Ness.

Craigmonie, the rocky hill to the rear of Lewiston and Drumnadrochit, was the scene of the last stand made by the Vikings in the early centuries, and the hill is still crowned with the remains of ancient fortifications. Tradition relates that Monie, son of the King

of Scandinavia, landed in Argyll with a large force, and accompanied
by his sister.

His retreat to the ships was cut off by the natives, and he was
chased northwards through the Caledonian valley until he reached
this district, and took refuge in Craigmonie. But the Norsemen were
finally driven to the plain below, and defeated with great slaughter.

Meantime, the young Princess took refuge in a crevice known as
Leabaidh-Nighean-an-Righ—the Bed of the King's Daughter; and
when the Highlanders were searching for their dead they found her,
but showed mercy, and she lived happily among them for many a
day. Her brother, however, was found in concealment and killed at
Corrimony.

Balmacaan—the Town of the Son of Hector—was the principal
possession of the MacLeans of Urquhart until about ninety years
ago, and when I visited it, the 150-year-old house lay quiet and
empty. The estate has changed hands several times in recent years
and was broken up and sold by the Seafields in 1945 to many
life-tenants and several "strangers," who had not even seen their
new property before the sale commenced.

After Culloden, the warriors of the Glen laid down their arms
outside Balmacaan House.

The hill behind Balmacaan is known as the Herd's Hill, and
long ago it was in part thickly populated with crofters. But the
crofters were evicted to make room for the rearing of pheasants, and
to turn the estate into a sporting one.

13. CASTLE AND KIRK

The district of Bunloit, like many another, is a mere shell of its former self, and where hundreds of hill cattle grazed on a multitude of crofts, just a few remain. It's the old story of emigration from these isolated places, so that "crofters," who still live on the heights, now only reside in the cottages, while the land stays untilled.

Nor can we altogether blame them, with a few inches of soil above hard rock.

General Wade's Military road from Inverness to Fort William passes over this hill, though now lost in the heather, and a quantity of cairns may suggest a fray or two in these parts.

A second place of interest in Bunloit is the Fort on the wooded hill at Wester Bunloit, which, I am told, was used as a refuge spot for hiding cattle when raiding parties came to the district from Lochaber. However, it may date further back than that.

Down on the main road again at Lewiston, we follow the Fort Augustus highway, past Borlum Farm, and reach Strone Point, where we find a few cottages and the ancient ruin of Castle Urquhart.

The Castle has rather a dull history, I consider, and dates into the 13th century. Perhaps even further back than that, as evidences of vitrification were found in these excavations.

It is said there was a royal fortalice at Urquhart in the reign of William the Lion, and that it passed from the hands of the Durwards to the Comyns, Lords of Badenoch. It played an important part in the Scottish Wars of Independence, and by a Royal Charter in 1509 passed into the hands of the Grants. In 1708 the country folk robbed the fort, by then uninhabited, of its woodwork and lead, until the law intervened; and in 1715 it was left a roofless structure by a great gust of wind. The looters even stole the dressed stone work, and parts of the Castle may still adorn some broken-down farmyard. In 1912 the ruins were handed over by the Seafield Trustees to the Commissioners of H.M. Works, in whose care they have since remained.

At Lower Lennie we get a magnificent view of John Cobb's Measured Mile, and it is here that the Glenurquhart folk have erected a monument to the great sportsman's memory on a small green patch by the roadside.

A little way on we reach Achnahannet—the Field of the Church; and, as the name suggests, an old Churchyard actually stood nearby. I believe it is on the lochside, though no visible traces of either kirk or tombstones remain to-day.

At Ruskich a small change-house was erected during the construction of Telford's road, and it won for itself a wild reputation. It is now merely a ruin by the roadside. Dr Johnson visited it on his travels.

According to legend, St Columba visited Invermoriston, and we find such places as St Columba's Well and St Columba's Churchyard, named after him, beside the village. The latter, *Clach Colum Chille*, is the community burying ground, beautifully situated in the centre of green pastures; but must not be confused with the smaller private burying ground of the Grants of Glenmoriston, erected by the last laird, and where only he and his wife lie at rest.

At the Well, near the smithy, St. Columba is believed to have preached, and this well has been noted for centuries for its curative properties. It is probable, too, that the saint founded the original Church.

The present kirk is not an old building, being erected in 1913 on the hill-side overlooking the village. A beautiful little Church with chairs instead of pews, it is quite unlike the usual type of ecclesiastical architecture we find in our Highland rural areas.

Opposite the manse and Church on the other side of the river lie a number of small crofts—Dalcattaig, Craigard and Redpark; and it was the latter which suffered most damage in the 1953 landslides. Freak thunderstorms hovered over the district for two days, causing several landslides, which tore down the wooded slopes of *Coille na Feinne*, destroying hundreds of trees. The largest of these slides completely swamped the fields of Redpark, ruining corn and potato crops, and, by a miracle, stopped within a few yards of four cottages.

Of the Seven Maidens of Port Clair, only four remain, as three of these great oak trees, believed to have been planted 350 years ago, have been cut down. According to a curse put on them when planted, a mishap should befall the man who put an axe to them, but nobody seems to know the fates of those who dared.

14. BRAVE DEEDS

I don't think I will ever forget my first journalistic visit to Glen-moriston, as on that specific occasion the heavens literally opened, and I was caught in the worst thunderstorm I have ever witnessed. It was the second freak storm in two days in that district. Three landslides had caused inestimable damage.

The first few miles of the Glen Moriston road are very badly surfaced, but improvements are underway now to cut off bad corners. Following the River Moriston, I think the first place of note we reach is the Pool of the Twenty Men, where a band of rustlers met their end when returning from one of their raids in the neighbour-hood. The incident occurred in mid-winter, when the river was frozen, and calling to an old woman on the other side, the raiders asked if the ice was strong enough to bear them. She replied in the affirmative, the attempt was made, but the ice broke, ending the careers of the twenty rogues. A memorial stone a few yards off the roadside, a little further along the road on the right, marks the grave of the woman, who, tradition relates, was buried near the pool as the result of considerable argument on the part of those who lived up and down the glen, as to the district in which her body should be buried.

There's still a division between Upper and Lower Glenmoriston, split from each other by wide open spaces, uninhabited and practically uncultivated.

Our next stop is to admire the view of the Upper Falls, one of the natural beauty spots of Glenmoriston. In fact, I am told that's where Moriston derives its name. It means "Big Falls."

Then where *Allt Iarairidh* (a small burn) joins the Moriston we find a number of burial cairns by the roadside between the road and the river, where funeral parties used to halt for a rest and refresh-ment when they came from a distance.

You can mark the path leading to the famous Footprints of Glenmoriston by the position of the second passing place on the road from Wester Dundreggan. Someone has built a small cairn on the edge of this path, and if you follow along it you will presently find a much larger cairn built up through the years by interested visitors. Behind this cairn you can see the two footprints, three inches deep, which have remained intact since as long ago as 1827.

The story of the Footprints is not one generally known, and originates from an incident which occurred during an outside service

WARDLAW MAUSOLEUM, KIRKHILL

Photo: J. S. Nairn

A RIVER BYPASSES A BRIDGE NEAR DUNEARN, NAIRNSHIRE

THE KIRK IN THE HOLLOW — ARDCLACH

RIVER FINDHORN

held at this spot. The preacher was an itinerant evangelist, Finlay
Munro, and during the service he was interrupted by two young
men, who, it is said, disapproved of his teachings and began to throw
mud at him, calling him a cheat and a liar.

The preacher closed his Holy Book, and, turning to his assailants,
declared that what he said was right, and, to prove it, he declared the
ground on which he stood would bear witness to the final day of
Judgment. His footprints remain to-day, and may quite easily stay
in this preserved condition for evermore!

Indeed, it is strange that the grass has grown to a depth of two
inches into these prints, but the third inch stays bare, just as the
evangelist prophesied. A birch tree also stood near the footprints,
but it was broken by a severe gale, and only a mark of its position
remains in evidence yet. However, according to the story, this tree
possessed three solitary branches, from which the Rev. Finlay took
his text—the Father, Son and Holy Ghost.

The bridge is interesting, as the pillars supporting it each contain
the sign of the Cross, put there at the request of a local keeper.
Connected with Torgyle Croft, formerly an inn, is the following
gruesome story, with rather a humorous touch.

A Highland piper retreating from Culloden was approaching the
inn, when he heard horse's hooves galloping behind him; and,
hiding behind a boulder, he slashed out with his sword when a
redcoated figure flashed by. The blow severed the soldier's head, and
the piper swooped on the body to retrieve any spoil. The boots of the
rider were the greatest temptation, but, try as he might, they would
not come off. However, not to be outdone, he took legs and all, and
continued on his way to the inn. Alas! no accommodation was
available, and he had to find lodgings in the byre, beside the
inn-keeper's cow.

Early next morning, when the dairymaid went out to milk the cow,
she saw the boots lying in the stall, and, unaware that the piper was
also sleeping in the byre, she ran back to the inn with the frightful
tale that the cow had eaten the traveller, and only his legs were
spared! However, before the true facts were known, the cow was shot
and buried!

An old legend of St Merchard, the patron saint of Glenmoriston,
relates how he was labouring in Strathglass with two missionaries,
when his attention was drawn to a white cow standing daily under a
certain tree. It never seemed to eat, yet always appeared well-fed.

Curiosity led him to dig the earth at the foot of the tree, where he
found three bells, new as from the maker's hands. Then, taking one
himself, and giving the others to his companions, he bade each go
his way and build a church on the site where his bell should ring for

the third time. One missionary went eastward and founded a church at Glenconvinth; the second west to Broadford in Skye; while St Merchard travelled south to Glenmoriston.

When he reached the hill, Suidhe Mhercheird (Merchard's Seat), the bell rang for the first time. It rang again at Merchard's Well; and the third time nearer the side of the River Moriston, where he founded a church.

For many years, until within living memory, the bell hung on a stone in the churchyard, and always rang of its own accord as a funeral approached! But eventually it was stolen by some labourers working in the vicinity, and its hiding-place never discovered.

Prince Charlie was in hiding in the district after Culloden, and although he is known to have spent a little while with the Seven Men of Glenmoriston in their cave at Corrie Doe, he must have found refuge in other similar caves in these bleak heather-clad hills.

Roderick MacKenzie was a loyal and trusted officer in the Jacobite army, and constantly by the side of the Prince, who on this occasion was in danger of being captured at any moment since the King's soldiers were gradually surrounding the cave in which they were concealed. Roderick quickly realised that something had to be done, and, as he bore a distinct resemblance to the Prince, decided on a plan.

And so, while sleeping in the cave, he was aroused by voices in the glen, and, going to the mouth of the cave, he could see figures of approaching Redcoats. Without a word he crept towards the sleeping Prince and quietly took his plaid and bonnet; then, having put them on, stole outside and down the glen.

When within firing distance of the Redcoats, he broke into the open and started to run. At once the soldiers spotted him and followed in pursuit, firing at him as they went; and as a bullet hit him he fell to the ground shouting:

"You've killed your Prince! You've killed your Prince."

Thinking him to be the Young Pretender, the soldiers immediately cut off his head and carried it in triumph to Fort Augustus, where they presented it to the Duke of Cumberland after Jacobite prisoners had identified it as the head of Prince Charlie. The Duke set off in haste for London, but it was soon discovered that a mistake had been made, as the Prince was found to be still at large!

Roadmen working nearby have greatly improved the approach to Roderick's cairn by placing concrete steps leading up to it. Unless you know where to look, you will not readily find his grave; but it is not very far away, across the road, on the bank of the River Moriston, distinctly marked under a mass of heather, with a bush of bog-myrtle growing at its head.

The cave at Corrie Doe where Prince Charlie was in hiding with the Seven Men of Glenmoriston, lies in the depths of *Coire Dho* away to the north, and is nine miles from Ceannacroc.

On the way up to the cave the explorer may come across some ruins of old settlements, but these have not been inhabited for over sixty years.

The story of the Seven Men of Glenmoriston is a fairly well-known tale, which does not really bear much repetition here. The Seven Men were all trained soldiers in Highland independent companies, although one of them, Grigor MacGregor, had actually been in Lord Loudon's army for the Government, and had deserted on the landing of the Prince.

Who were these Seven Men? Their names are given as Hugh, Alexander and Donald Chisholm, sons of Paul Chisholm, Blairie; Alexander Macdonald, Aonach; John Macdonald, Craskie; Grigor MacGregor and Patrick Grant, Craskie. Having witnessed the slaughter of their friends and relations, the burning of their homes and loss of their property, they bound themselves together and vowed never to surrender themselves or their arms to the English. Many are the tales of their daring raids on enemy stores and interceptions of Redcoat patrols; but their greatest hour came when they were privileged to hide their Prince and keep him out of harm's way.

One of these Seven Men, Hugh Chisholm of Blairie, afterwards went to live in Edinburgh. He would never give his right hand to anybody after saying farewell to the Prince in Corrie Doe; and Glenmoriston tradition goes even further and relates that he never afterwards washed that lucky right hand, which was heartily shaken by his own lawful king.

15.   FORT AUGUSTUS

Approaching Fort Augustus from Inverness, we find rather an unusual island about a hundred yards from the shore of Loch Ness, called Cherry Island. It was built as a fort by the Frasers, and, as now it appears comparatively small, and covered with a handful of trees, you may well wonder how more than a single family ever managed to take refuge on it.

However, tradition relates that it was formerly much larger, and, at the building of the Caledonian Canal, Loch Ness was raised nine feet and most of the original island is to-day underwater.

Of course, you may think it strange that I say the Frasers "built" this island; normally, we do not usually "build" islands. Most of them are natural. But this island is artificial, and was set up on logs as a retreat in times of clan strife.

Near the end of the Auchterawe road, and on our right, stands the stately mansion of Inchnacardoch, until a few years ago a shooting lodge, and during the last war requisitioned by the army.

Auchterawe Farm has been taken over by the Forestry Commission but at the furthest point of this road we find an old burying-ground, only used by families with lairs; and overlooking it is the wooded crag of Tomdhune, with the remains of a vitrified fort on its heights.

The house, reputed to be the oldest in Fort Augustus, is at Inveroich Point, and it was once inhabited by the commandant of the galley which plied up and down the loch. In these early days, there were several houses at the Point, but apparently three of them have been joined together to form a single building, now known as Inveroich House.

The middle portion is said to have been a brewery, used only for private distilling.

These buildings all belonged to the War Department a hundred years ago, and of interest is the step at the back door of Inveroich House with an arrow head and W.D. 1857 carved on it. The Canal Company bought the houses from the War Department along with the land for the construction of the canal, and gradually they fell into private ownership. Incidentally, the old main road crosses the Oich a little way from Inveroich House, though the bridge (half of wood and half of stone) is only open for pedestrians. Most of this bridge was carried away in the flood of 1849, which caused much damage in the north at the time.

If you take a stroll down to Inveroich Point, you will see all that remains of one of the last Loch Ness steamers, the *Gairlochy*, which took fire on a stormy night while anchored at the pier. The crew managed to take her a little way out from the pier into shallow water, where she burnt out and became a total loss. Most of the hulk was later cut away with acetylene burners, but a couple of feet of the hulk still rises above the loch's surface.

Bun Oich is just a little community by itself, and was founded in 1779 by a Fraser of Culduthel, and formerly known as Frasertown. The story goes that Fraser was envious of the prosperity of the folk who lived under the shadow of the Fort, and was anxious to secure similar privileges and advantages for his own clansmen.

To the rear of Bun Oich is Battery Rock, from where Jacobite troops bombarded the Fort, and with a successful shot struck the powder magazine and blew that portion of the Fort sky-high, causing the garrison to surrender to Prince Charlie two days later.

Another place of interest in Fort Augustus is the old King's Inn, which witnessed many a drunken brawl and deeds of blood and lawlessness. It was first built as an hotel in the early days of General Wade's roads, but has been repaired and renovated since then.

To-day we find a thriving little community in Fort Augustus with a host of good shops.

Kilcumein Churchyard, lying in a sheltered corner by the borders of the River Tarff, is believed to have been the site of the original foundation of Kilcumein and the ancient parish chapel; but the graveyard was not enclosed until 1796. Just outside the wall lies buried the son and heir of Archibald Fraser of Abertarff, the great-grandson of Lord Lovat of the '45, who, it is said, died before his parents. Having lost his heir, an only son, the father was not merely grieved but embittered, and to "spite the Almighty" had the boy buried outside the holy precincts!

In this graveyard lies the dust of John Anderson, hero of Burn's famous song: "John Anderson, my Jo, John."

So we find ourselves at the gateway of another great glen—Glengarry—a glen full of lore, romance and bravery. Its story would fill another volume. We've travelled far enough, and here we must part; but if ever you call for a chat at any of these wayside places we have visited together, I feel sure you will receive, as I have done, a real, sincere Highland welcome.

16. CLACHNAHARRY

One of my favourite views is from a point on the main north road on the boundary of Clachnaharry. It is a view of the Beauly Firth, which the motorist approaches quite suddenly as he takes the double bend over the railway bridge.

The picturesque hamlet of Clachnaharry, less than a mile north-west of Inverness, at the mouth of the Caledonian Canal, seems a haven of peace and quiet in these busy days, and the scene from the high road is indeed a sight that many a Highlander in alien lands remembers with a thrill in his heart.

When the tide is out, long stretches of muddy sand sweep across to the farthermost shores of the Black Isle, and only the central channel shatters the monotony of the firth's sea-bed. In the background looms Ben Wyvis, seldom without a powdering of snow.

At the head of the firth nestles Beauly in the lap of Dunmore, while on a clear day the hills of Strathglass steal into the picture. On the left of this view the Great North Road winds along the water's edge until it disappears from sight in the woodlands of Bunchrew.

I like to stake a claim on this vision, as before me lies an area which I have grown to know and love; a district which is practically undiscovered by the tourist who merely uses it as a stepping-stone to some other beauty spot. Perhaps we do not have the majesty of the west, with its incomparable grandeur, but we do have a countryside steeped in history and soaked in tales of romance and devilry, with a sprinkling here and there of modern enterprise.

Until about forty years ago Clachnaharry was an independent village, but since then has been included in the burgh boundary of Inverness. The occasion, I believe, was the installation of water and electricity from the town's supplies. However, apart from these associations many of the villagers still like to think themselves a separate community. I remember one year some of the enterprising folk staged a gala week, bedecked houses and thoroughfare with bunting and flags; paraded through the Highland Capital; and succeeded in showing up the town!

One of the oldest buildings is the former toll house, which recalls the days when passing traffic was taxed to support the upkeep of the roads when daily coaches ran instead of trains.

There's a good smuggling story associated with Clachnaharry Inn which is rather amusing and throws an unusual light on the manners of former days. The main character in the plot is none other than a badly-off country minister, Master Alastair Hutchison, of Kiltarlity, who was reputed to be one of the most pious and Godly men one could wish to meet.

In his day smuggling was fairly rife, and according to his creed he preached against it in a general way. Yet in spite of his preachings he kept his own private still at the back of the manse, and using his glebe grown barley he would brew his own "droppie" whisky, arguing that it was within his right to increase, where possible, his small savings. Nevertheless, he prayed constantly that the eyes of the exciseman would never alight on him.

On one occasion he sold his whisky to an Inverness publican, and arranged to bring it into the town sometime during the week. However, for some obscure reason the publican informed the Customs officer, who lay in wait for him at Clachnaharry. About midnight a horse-drawn cart laden with peat drew into the village, and the exciseman appeared from his hiding place and grabbed the reins.

"Where are you going to at this time of night?" he called to the shabbily-dressed driver.

"To town with my peats," was the reply.

"Indeed, sir! But first you must let me search your load," said the officer, and proceeded to remove the top layers of peat. Soon several concealed casks were brought to light.

"Oh, Lord, thou hast betrayed me at last!" lamented the old minister, and poured out his woeful tale. The officer was a fair man, and decided to let him go, and horse and cart were presently jogging on their way towards Inverness.

The whisky was left with rather an astonished publican, and the minister returned on his homeward way; but the casks of liquor had not even been taken down to the cellar before the exciseman pounced on the publican and confiscated the lot!

On a promontory overlooking the Firth stands a memorial of a clan feud. One gale accounted for a winged figure standing on a column of stone, and another removed the column, so that now only the base is left. The gale damage has caused considerable ill-feeling in the village, as the Town Council of Inverness have never made any steps to restore the monument since its first collapse. Before the Second World War the newspapers carried a story about "a grey lady" who haunted it, but like so many other "grey ladies" who have appeared elsewhere, she was soon forgotten and regarded as a trick of the imagination.

Yet there is no reason why ghosts should not haunt these parts, as it was near this village of Clachnaharry that one of the fiercest clan battles of the dark ages took place, between the MacKintoshes and the Munroes.

The story is an interesting one, and history records that in the year 1378 the young laird of Fowlis, John Munro, was returning home from a business expedition to the south, when he chanced to rest the night with his entourage on the lands of Strathardel, near Blair Atholl in Perthshire. Overnight, as his horses grazed, the owners of the grass, whose permission had not been sought, crept stealthily up to the steeds and without exception docked their tails. In those days a horse's tail swept to the ground and was a thing of beauty much to be cherished. A short tail was considered absurd.

Not unnaturally the next morning Munro of Fowlis and his friends were furious at the sight of their horses, and Munro himself wanted revenge there and then, but his clansmen counselled caution as they were outnumbered, and persuaded him not to do anything at the moment. So they continued on their way.

On his arrival home, Munro singled out three hundred and fifty of his strongest and fittest men and taking with them suitable provisions, they set off to the lands of Strathardel.

Announcing the reason for his return, he began to ravage the district, meeting little resistance, and triumphantly his men drove away all horses and cattle they could lay hands on.

Their return journey took them through the lands of Moy, the hereditary home of the MacKintoshes, and according to the country custom they were approached to pay toll duty in kind. The Laird of Moy sent out three of his clansmen and demanded a portion of the travellers' goods, so Munro selected a third part of the cattle and offered them in payment. MacKintosh would have been content with his share, but his clansmen begged him to ask for more, at least one-half of the total spoil.

This excessive demand did not please the Munroes, and without more ado they gathered together their belongings and set off as quickly as possible without leaving any share at all. Meanwhile the unhappy MacKintosh, urged on by his followers, mustered as many men as he could gather and gave chase. But it was only within the outskirts of Inverness that they suceeded in catching up with the Munroes, who had the advantage of being on the other side of the River Ness.

John Munro sent the stolen animals home with fifty of his men, and with the remainder of the little army prepared for the onslaught.

The two clans met in battle at Clachnaharry, and soon after the start of the fray the Laird of Moy was killed, along with his brother and second son. Many of the Munroes were slain, but they finally won the day, and it is said that more than two hundred MacKintoshes lost their lives.

John Munro was severely wounded and was left on the battlefield as dead, but the next morning he was rescued by an old woman from Clunes, and, after being given food, he was taken to the Lovat country where he was able to recover. this act laid a foundation of friendship between the two clans of Fraser and Munro.

Thus the monument to the great battle—a memorial to a band of gallant Highlandmen who fell fighting for their name and honour—as they conceived it.

The road from Inverness to Beauly is familiar to all those who travel it frequently, but the impression one gets from a motor car is the sparseness of the population. Only an occasional cottage or farm steading interrupts the beauty of the Highland countryside; yet away from the roadside, almost within a stone's throw, live a colony of crofters who in generations have built up the fertility of their meagre acres and have formed the backbone of a thriving community.

When we leave Clachnaharry behind us and travel along the Great North Road, passing the Delmore Roadhouse, our first call is at Bunchrew, the outpost of the parish of Kirkhill, and the boundary of the Lovat estate. A few years ago we could have known our presence in Bunchrew blindfold by the "humpy back" bridge, a horror to the speedy motorists. I hope in time the County Council will dispense with all these obstacles on the main thoroughfares, and already steps have been taken to remove the most treacherous. They lowered the road at Bunchrew by six feet, and it is now similar in width and surface to a first-class highway.

I have come across several Kirktons in the north. It is a common name, but I think the Kirkton at Bunchrew is pretty widely known. The late Kenneth MacGillivray, whom I knew well, bred his famous herd of Shorthorn cattle on this farm, and the strain has won many honours and high credit in foreign lands as well as at home. His daughter Jean farmed Phopachy for a few years before his death, and after Kirkton was taken over by the laird, Lord Lovat, she took up residence there.

The Kirkton steading was built on the old kirk site of Fernua, but only a few tombstones now mark the spot. The nearby village of Englishton is no longer to be seen, but the muir on the hill is still well in evidence, with a thriving community of crofters seeking a livelihood from their small acreages. The derivation of Fernua, I am told is "the place of the alder," a tree common to the district, which is generally found near a burn, being grouped in a family of water-loving arbors.

The burn at Fernua is the Kirkton burn, which divides the two muirs of Kirkton and Bunchrew, while farther east the Bunchrew burn (which formerly flowed under the "Humpy Bridge,") is the dividing line of the estates of Bunchrew and Lovat. The remnants of a stone dyke following the twists and turns of the Bunchrew burn suggests that labour in these old days was both cheap and plentiful.

Bunchrew House dates back to the 17th century, and part of it is the oldest existing edifice hereabout. It has been in the family of Fraser-Mackenzie for well over a hundred years. The family still live there, but only inhabit one-fifth of the building, the remainder being divided into four separate service flats, a fate which has befallen so many other big mansions, no longer an asset to the Highland laird. Here President Forbes was born.

A site of a battle is marked on the survey map as Blar-na-leine — the Field of the Swamps—and there is ample evidence of this with at least a dozen cairns, now practically lost in Englishton Wood; but I'm afraid I cannot find any definite information about the battle. The plantation was cut down in the First World War by German prisoners, and replanted about the same time.

At the end of last century a small kirk was built by the roadside at Bunchrew, which served the community and came under the wing of the established church at Kirkhill. It is not a very beautiful building, a common fault with our Highland churches, and it has a membership of fifty folk.

Small though Bunchrew may be, it is at least independent compared with Lentran, two miles away, where the older folk still remember a meal mill, bobbin mill, blacksmith's shop and police station; but to-day we find none of them.

The name Lentran means "the meadow of the corncrakes" and they often used to be heard in the neighbourhood, though not so frequently lately.

17. REELIG TO BEAULY

A popular landmark in the parish of Kirkhill is Bogroy Inn, which has been closely associated with smugglers in the not so distant past. Until the end of the 19th century illicit whisky distilling appears to have been fairly prevalent in the Inverness district, and there were ample opportunities for the glen folk to keep their private "stills" with little risk of interference from the nosey excisemen. In fact, I sometimes wonder if the art is altogether dead in the many out-of-the-way crofts in the hills.

As long as the smugglers avoided detection from the Customs officers, who periodically paid visits and made raids on suspected "bothies," whisky making was quite profitable.

A quarter of barley cost about a pound to purchase, but many of these clandestine distillers grew their own crops. From a quarter of grain they obtained about fifteen gallons of whisky, which in those days sold at eighteen shillings a gallon, a considerable difference from present day rates.

Of course much of the whisky was drunk by the community themselves which led to a considerable amount of squalor and drunkenness, but perhaps as much as £10 or more might have been made from the mere cost of the barley.

The most famous tale connected with Bogroy Inn and smuggling days is the one in which a cask of confiscated whisky was stolen under the very eyes of the excisemen.

After the confiscation, the smugglers followed the customs men to the Inn, and being on friendly terms with the servant girl, got her to tell them where the cask had been placed in their room. An augur bored a hole in the ceiling of the room below, directly beneath the cask and by this means the whisky was retrieved. The hole can still be seen, and a framed account of the incident hangs in a small recess beside it, with the satirical note that whisky is no longer stored in the room upstairs!

There's another tale connected with Bogroy Inn, in which Customs officers raided a barn in Strathglass where a known quantity of milk was stored. The smugglers, however, were determined to save their pricious supplies, and barricaded the door of the barn. Being made of wicker-work, it had not much strength, so it was not difficult for one of the officers to thrust his cutlass through it, and pierce a man in the chest.

Fearing the damage they had done, the officers set off, but in their hurry one of them tripped and fell, and the pursuing offenders trampled him underfoot. The injured man was carried to the inn at Bogroy where he died two days later as the result of his injuries.

At Bogroy, a "B" road turns off, opposite a war memorial, to Kirkhill, and re-joins the main road again at Conon-bank, thus providing a short-cut to the north. Before continuing on our journey towards Beauly, I would like to depart from our route and visit Kirkhill and neighbouring lands.

The road passes by Kingillie and Newton, with the scattered village of Kirkhill at the top of the hill, one mile from Bogroy.

I have already mentioned the kirk of Fernua at Bunchrew, which was one of the original churches in the parish. On a small hillock north of the village are the ruins of another old kirk, Wardlaw, and it was with the union of the parishes of Fernua and Wardlaw that the parish of Kirkhill was formed. Originally the church of the western parish stood at Dunballoch, on the Beauly road, but in the 13th century under an agreement between the Bishop of Moray and John Bisset of Lovat, it was transferred to this beautiful hillock overlooking the rich lands of Lovat.

The name "Wardlaw" is derived from ward-law or watch hill, and presumably was a look-out for invading armies in the days of clan strife.

According to the author of the Wardlaw MS., which has been admirably edited from the original manuscript by the late Dr. William MacKay of Inverness, the old church at Dunballoch was dedicated to St Mauritius, and the new church which was set up on Wardlaw was dedicated to the Virgin Mary. Hence, it has come about that the hillock has been named Cnoc Moire, or Mary's Hill.

The old church of Cnoc-Moire was abandoned in 1790, when the present kirk was built on a less interesting site in the centre of the village, though I doubt if the present village was there then.

In the year 1635 the Lovat mausoleum was built on Cnoc-Moire, and until 1815 the Lovat chiefs were buried in its vaults. Since then it has fallen into disuse, and one can only gain entrance if in possession of the key. the floor has sunk in places, and in the vault below, the outer casings of the coffins are badly broken. Fallen from their shelves, many of the coffins are strewn untidily on the floor.

The belfry of the mausoleum, similar to the Tower of St Duthus at Tain, may have been designed by the same architect, and belongs to the 17th century. Among the relics of the past which are still preserved in the building is a fragment of an old bell, but the upper part has been broken and is missing. According to the Wardlaw MS. that bell was taken from Beauly Priory and, being too large for the steeple, was hung for a time on wooden supports on the knoll to the

south-east of the churchyard. It was afterwards recast in Holland
and made smaller. In its new cast it was set up in the belfry in 1635
and bore the inscription "Michael Burgerhous mi fecit anno d.
1634."

To-day only an occasional funeral disturbs the serenity of the
ancient burying ground, but away back from the past come stories of
high festivities at the burials of the Lovat Chiefs, attended by as
many as 8,000 clansmen. Now their family burying ground is at
Eskadale.

There's an interesting account in the Wardlaw MS. of the trial of
witches by one Paterson the Pricker, who practised rather a crude
method of discovering their "guilt."

He first stripped his victims naked, then polled their heads and hid
the hair in a recess of a stone wall. After rubbing his hands over the
whole body he inserted a long brass pin right up to its head. Then, in
the author's words: "with shame and fear being dashed, they felt it
not, but he left it in the flesh, deep to the head, and desired them to
find and take it out!" Presumably, if the pin could not be found, it
was a confession of guilt, and several who were never brought to
confession died in prison.

After several years Paterson's true guise as an imposter came to
light; he was unmasked and proved to be a woman dressed in man's
clothing.

To the east of Wardlaw lie the farmlands of Clunes and Groam,
while Easter and Wester Lovat across the marches share a similar
heavy clay soil. There are decided proofs of the depression and
upheaval of the land, and actual proof of reclamation from the
sea of much of the soil in the parish is shown by the reeds growing
inland which normally so luxuriantly grow by the sea-shore.

The flat lands of the Lovats, Clunes and Groam, I understand,
were all reclaimed from the firth, the present railway line being built
where the sea once lapped against the shore. Shell beds have been
found well above high water mark, and at the east end of the railway
bridge at Clunes, ten feet above the rails of the Highland line. Burial
cairns have also been noticed in the Beauly Firth, which point to a
time when part of it must have been dry land.

Incidentally the name "Clunes" is fairly common in the north,
and is found in various forms, such as Clunas, Cluny, Clune, and
Cluanie. It is derived from the Gaelic word meaning "a green
place."

But Clunes is not the original name of this 265 acre estate. Old

Note—Wardlaw Kirkyard was the scene of one of the last trials by
ordeal in Scotland.

maps still give it as Fingask, and I believe some of the older folk preserve the former and more attractive name of Fingask, which was changed in memory of a former home by a previous proprietor, Donald Cameron, when he came from Clunes in Lochaber.

* * *

Returning to the main road at Bogroy, we follow it round by Reelig and Moniack, interesting in the fact .that the estates both belong to Frasers, the family name of the district, usually designated "the Lovat Country."

You will not find the name Reelig on the very old maps, as formerly the mansion house was known as Easter Moniack. It was practically rebuilt in 1830, but incorporates part of an earlier building about a century older. The original "duchus" was something more primitive still; and the laird's family occupied a modest dwelling at Rebeg, built in 1708.

Throughout the greater part of the 18th and 19th centuries, the lairds of Reelig and their sons sought their fortunes in the East and West Indies and elsewhere abroad. Two were well-known orientalists, and one of these, James Baillie Fraser (1783-1850), in his retirement, laid out the present Reelig garden. He and his father devoted much of their time to planting the Reelig Glen, now the property of the Forestry Commission.

Some fine cedars of lebanon in the Reelig garden were planted in 1783, and also amid the floral scene is a large stone cairn, which Major Fraser tells me is almost certainly prehistoric, and is known as the "Giant's Grave."

"In 1799 someone—probably an amateur antiquary—told my great-great-grandmother that it was a Viking's grave," he says, but it decidedly is not. However, the old lady was so elated by this piece of news that she pulled down the cairn and rebuilt part of it in the shape of a boat. It has never been excavated, and there is no reason whatsoever to believe that it is anything out of the ordinary. I should much prefer it left in peace."

There are several ruins in the Reelig estate, and I think the best known one is Tigh-an-Aigh (pronounced Tan-eye), the house of good luck, or fortune, which is supposed to have been built in the "hungry times" of 1846 when there was a universal failure of the potato crops. With the object of giving employment to his tenants and others on the estate, the laird arranged for the construction of this building, but when the workers returned to their labours each morning they found what had been built the day before had been entirely pulled down overnight.

Of course, they blamed the fairies, but I understand the laird himself was responsible, in order to keep the folk employed.

The names on the higher ground of Reelig are interesting, and show that the raising of horses was a local industry. Three examples are: *Meall-na-Caiplich*—the Foal's or Filly's Hill; *Meall-na-Caiplich moire*—the Mare's Hill; and *Faschapple*—the Mare's pasture or homestead.

Quite close to Rebeg Farm is an old lime quarry which was regularly operated in the 60's and 70's of the last century.

* * *

Neighbouring Reelig Hill, we find the crofters of Clunes, not to be confused with the other Clunes of Fingask. But interesting is the fact that this district is believed to be the original home of the Clan Macrae before they evacuated to the west, to Kintail on Loch Duich.

It must be hundreds of years ago since the Wild Macraes settled in these parts, and it is of interest historically that nineteen years ago while ploughing one of his fields, James Forbes, of No. 6 South Clunes, made a discovery. At one point in the field the soil appeared to sink, so fetching a punch from his steading he prodded the ground, and later unearthed a treasure, which at the time brought momentary fame to his humble abode.

His discovery was the skeleton of a man, lying on one side with knees bent, and beside him, an urn which had probably been grasped under his arm pit. The sides, end and top of his tomb were stone flagged, and when Professor Low from Aberdeen came over to examine and remove the bones, he claimed that in all probability they were over two thousand years old. By the position in which the skeleton lay, he considered that it was a chief, as no ordinary person would have been buried thus.

Long ago the present district of Clunes was formerly part of Caiplich, and the original Clunes began nearer Knockbain.

On the survey map you will find Castle Sponie, close to the croft of Leanach, and within the holding's boundaries. Actually it was a spying fort used by the Clan Fraser to detect the presence of approaching enemies, and under such circumstances fires were lit as a warning.

Moniack Castle is believed to date back to the 16th century, built by the Lovat family, probably the present Strichen branch, cousins of the old stock. It is known that at the time of the '45, Simon, Lord Lovat, removed all his valuables to Moniack, fearing they might be stolen and thus they were able to be preserved to modern times. "My Tower of Moniack" was the name he gave the Castle.

* * *

A popular bus fare stage on the Inverness-Beauly road is Brochies Corner, where the Kiltarlity road branches off but the identity of "Brochie" is rather a controversial point.

Only a fragment of a gable end of an old change-house—where the traveller also changed his breath—is still visible in the wood on the right-hand side of the road going north, but whether this wayside inn was once owned by a man named Brochie, or not, I cannot say. I believe the Gaelic speaking folk had another name for the corner— Brochies House, which rather suggests this solution. Another belief is based on the Gaelic word *Brocs,* meaning "badger," and the idea has arisen that there was once a badger's earth in the vicinity. I'm inclined to believe the latter.

About a mile from the village of Beauly is Beauly Bridge, and beside it on the west bank of the river you will find the old Corff House, unique in being one of the few corff houses left in the north. Built in 1742, by Simon, Lord Lovat, it was re-roofed from thatch and slated by High Commissioner Alastair Fraser in 1808.

Before the introduction of railways into the Highlands, salmon caught in the river were half boiled in large copper boilers, salted and put into kegs, then dispatched by boat to Holland, where they met a ready market. Of course, in those days the fishermen lacked the knowledge of sea netting they have to-day, so that the rivers simply swarmed with fish, and a catch of 50,000 salmon was quite a common haul in a season. Now most of them are netted along the coast.

For fifty years Alex Macrae was head fisherman and water bailiff on the Beauly, whose duties included full charge of the angling and netting from Chanonry Point, Fortrose, to the head of Strathglass.

I remember him telling me that the biggest fish he had ever seen hooked weighed 50 lbs., and that was caught by a guest at Beaufort Castle in 1904.

The former Beauly Bridge was destroyed by the great flood of 1892, caused by a thaw which melted a tremendous quantity of snow. The river rose so high that the impact of the water against the bridge made it collapse. Pits of turnips and stacks of hay were swept away, and the crofters of Redcastle on the other side of the Beauly Firth reaped an unexpected harvest on the shore!

Mary Queen of Scots wasn't far wrong when, on a visit to Beauly, she looked out of a window in the Priory on a glorious summer morning and exclaimed: "Beau lieu." Some folk believe this is the true derivation of the place name. At least it is quite a nice idea, but long before this royal lady ever lived the village was in existence, which rather outrules this picturesque tradition.

The monks of long ago called it "bellus locus"—beautiful place—

a more likely origin though the meaning is the same, and the present modern village is built on the site of the orchard and grounds of the old priory.

Until the First World War the village harbour on the River Beauly was still used by vessels up to 150 tons, and farmers exported their produce from it. Imports were coal and lime.

It was due to the export of cereals that a minor rebellion nearly took place in the village in 1848. In this year there was a great scarcity of grain, and farmers were fetching a high price for it in southern markets, which was duly shipped from Beauly pier. However, gangs of youths met the carts bringing the bulk grain to the harbour, and unyoking the horses, they tipped the produce into the river, rather than see it being sent elsewhere. The Sheriff arrived on the scene and read the Riot Act, but it had no effect and eventually troops had to be sent from Fort George to quell the disturbance.

Only remnants of the old harbour can now be seen, in a decayed state, overgrown with weeds, and an eyesore to the local inhabitants.

Ships coming up the river required a pilot, as the river bed conditions changed every year, and I remember hearing one story of a German boat, whose skipper grudged paying the pilot fees, and decided to use his own skill in manoeuvering his ship into the Firth. How wrong he was! His vessel had scarcely sailed fifty yards before it grounded, and eventually became a total wreck within a stone's throw of the pier.

The Priory at Beauly was founded in 1230 by John Bisset, a member of the English family of that name whose ancestors came over with William the Conqueror. The Priory is one of the three Valliscaulian Order houses ever to be established in the British Isles, and is now only a ruin.

One of the best known stories told around the Priory is about the tailor and the bloodless hand, which I understand has been associated with many other similar places, in history.

One evening after village politics had had their turn in a local inn, the question of the tailor's professional abilities were brought up; so to test his courage the shoemaker wagered with him that he could not finish a pair of trousers inside the Priory within a given time. The tailor accepted the wager and proceeded with his tools and candle into the Priory, took his seat on a gravestone, and set to work.

Suddenly he heard a deep stern voice behind him:

"Behold, tailor, the hand without flesh or blood rising up behind you!" it said.

"I see that," retorted the tailor, "but I must continue with my work!"

The voice repeated the same frightful words, and the hand came nearer and nearer, yet the brave little tailor continued until the last stitch was finished.

Then he grabbed his gear and fled as fast as he could, with the ghostly hand in hot pursuit. It had just overtaken him as he rushed out of the west door, when it made a furious clutch in his direction. However, it missed the poor little man and instead took a piece out of the moulding of the door, and the mark of the five fingers can still be seen to this day although now partially obliterated by a knock from a workman's wheelbarrow.

Another story associated with the Priory has a connection with smuggling days, and it concerns a phantom rider who was alleged to be seen galloping down Croyard Road, through the village square, and disappearing into the grounds of the Priory. At least that's the story which went round the doorsteps, keeping folk well indoors after dark.

By a strange coincidence local excisemen had confiscated large quantities of malt from neighbouring "bothies" and had stored it in a cellar of the Lovat Arms Hotel, now the Bank of Scotland buildings, until a date was fixed to hold a public auction.

With the terror of the phantom rider echoing through the village it is not unnatural that there were no eye witnesses on the streets when thieves broke into the hotel and stole the whole contents of confiscated malt. By the way, the phantom rider was never seen again!

To-day the old Priory forms no part in village life, and remains what it is—a ruin. In fact, few of the younger generation acknowledge its existence, and whereas Beauly was once a great ecclesiastical centre it is now a hub of tradesmen and the passing show of motor cars travelling north and south.

Beauly might have been known for its spa, had the thrill of its own mineral well, opened by Lord Lovat in 1895, not died a natural death. The water had therapeutic value, containing sodium and magnesium salts in the form of sulphates and chlorides, and there were various legends of folk crippled with rheumatism finding health from those waters and throwing away their crutches. The well at Bridgend is practically forgotten by many of the Beauly people, though I did hear a rumour recently that the village council might resuscitate its vanished glories.

Above Beauly is Dun Mor—big hill—with an unrivalled view, and the village lies in the shadow of Cnoc-na-Rath with a varied selection of derivations. Some say it means Hill of the People or Hill of the Fairies. Other explanations are Hill of Wrath, or Hill of the Fort. The Brahan Seer prophesied that Cnoc-na-Rath would one day descend into the centre of Beauly, which suggested that the village would surely extend. However, it is now believed that the prophesy has already been fulfilled as the road metal used in the building of Beauly Square, originated from its boulders and pebbles.

18.   HIGHLAND MARKETS

The Inverness Wool Fair is one of the highlights of country life in the Highlands and takes place every year during the second week of July. But as time has changed modes of fashion, so has it given a new look to a gathering of rural folk who once escaped from the glens and hillside to a grand reunion of friends, and to freely sell and buy produce and stock. It was a great day! The menfolk were chiefly interested in their wool clips and came to meet the big wool brokers from the south, while their women brought butter, cheese, crowdie and eggs in the hope of swelling their meagre earnings.

Of course there were sales too of ewes and lambs, but not as we know them to-day in saleyards and sawdust rings. The selling was left to the individual who parted with his beasts by private deals.

It was a three day event compared with the one at present, and was held in Church Street, outside what is now the Caledonian Hotel. Then it changed over to the Station Square, while in Bank Street (now a parking stance) the "horsey" folk gathered with their steeds and conducted their sales on similar lines.

In 1905 the auctioneering firm of Hamilton, Sim and Shivas was established, and they started a rival sale in their yards, which eventually drew both crowds and horses from the centre of the town, and so began a new era, with horses a bigger attraction on Wool Fair day than sheep.

Even in the few years we have lived in the north, I remember some great horse sales. There was over three hundred entries at one of them, and I heard afterwards that only a handful of horses which passed under James Barclay's baton that day were sound! Yet the turnover was terrific. The Clydesdales were sold in the railway yard beside the cattle truck sidings, while the garrons and ponies occupied the crowded smoky sale ring during the best part of the morning and afternoon. Mr Barclay's voice was reduced to a silent croak before the finish!

Across the way at MacDonald, Fraser & Company's auction mart, a new Wool Fair had begun to take shape in the form of attested cattle. After the war the Highlands became more and more "tuberculin-tested" minded, until now nearly every dairy herd has passed the test. Some neighbouring counties are nearly 100 per cent. clean.

At the 1952 Wool Fair cattle entries exceeded 250 head, while horses at Hamilton's had dwindled to a mere hundred. Another sign of the times!

The Wool Fair Concert was a popular social event and for years was run by the Inverness Strathspey and Reel Society under the direction of the late Alex. Grant, a master of the fiddle, and a farmer himself at Tomnahurich farm (now a housing site). But on his death the Society discontinued their entertainments, and during the war the Inverness Farmers' Society took over the organising of a Gaelic-English concert in connection with the Scottish Agricultural Red Cross Fund.

Two local newspapers brought out special Wool Fair editions, and the *Wool Fair Circular,* on sale on the Friday night and Saturday morning, featured the prices gained and buyers and salesmen present.

The old-time custom of private bargaining brings to mind the famous monthly markets held at Muir of Ord which were in force since about 1820 until 1908. The market site is now an excellent golf course, but the sales are still remembered by those "on the other side of fifty."

The moor where the markets were held originally belonged to the monks of Beauly Priory.

Making use of the cattle tracks over the hills, drovers brought cattle to and from Falkirk, at that time the biggest market town of its kind in Scotland. They thought nothing of a fortnight's walk, whereas nowadays the youngsters will scarcely walk their way to school!

Time may have transformed the old market stance into a golf course, but nevertheless it has not completely destroyed the few remaining features of these occasions. On the right hand side of the main road travelling north is a "street" of houses which once comprised the former Caledonian Bank, the Commercial Bank, and an eating house, while nearer Beauly is another eating house, now named Lovat Cottage. Its front porch was once the auctioneer's stand when bidding was in practice near the close of these markets.

The existing golf club house was a former public house, and I am told there were four others, wooden erections, now demolished. Opposite the bank on the other side of the road the market water pump is still in use, and octogenarian Neil MacDonald, who lived in a former eating house, tells me that he remembers buying water from this pump at a halfpenny a glass!

Special trains were run to the markets, and a platform nearby enabled passengers to alight and facilitated the loading and unloading of stock.

The Muir of Ord Market was a two-day event, with the sheep sales on a Wednesday and the horses and cattle the next day. The school children enjoyed a general holiday and were engaged by the farmers to help herd the sheep and cattle and keep them from straying. The main road knew less traffic in those days, and the horse dealers could show off their paces with little interference.

Feeing markets have also faded into the past and the Lammas mart at Beauly, held on the 12th August, was an opportunity for local farmers to take on harvest workers. At the Wool Fair shepherds were engaged, but special feeing markets were held in Inglis Street, Inverness, in February, May and November. The February market was for married men only, as presumably they required more time to get ready to shift camp.

Government control of wool before the last war, terminated all business deals of wool clips between farmer and broker, and similarly the standstill order of labour, brought to an end the feeing markets. The country markets were ousted by the introduction of auctioneering firms, and the Muir of Ord markets especially seemed to fade out after auction marts were established in Dingwall. However, it has been pointed out to me that the auctioneers would have made a wiser choice had they set up business nearer the old market stance at Muir of Ord, as the railway facilities are better, with a station equipped with all the necessary sidings. In Dingwall, stock has to be herded or otherwise transported through the streets. However, it is too late now!

19. HIGHLAND FERRY

The shore road to Kessock branches off the main Fortrose road at the Garguston Farm cottages, in the centre of the pretty little parish of Killearnan. Redcastle, the home of the Baillies for more than a century, is believed to be the oldest inhabited castle in Scotland. Just beside it is the tiny village called Milton of Redcastle, which once was a thriving community itself, with two pubs, a shop, tailor, carpenter, miller, sawmiller and blacksmith, and you could get nearly everything you wanted there without going elsewhere. Now it is a home of rest for retired estate workers with only one shop and the ghosts of the past to keep them amused.

Seventy years ago we might have attended a capital village market at Redcastle, but now the market place has been converted into gardens for the villagers. The old stance is situated between the two rows of cottages, some of them still thatched, though the art of thatching is quickly dying.

West of the village is Quarry of Redcastle, also housing estate workers, and remnants of a pier can still be seen jutting out into the firth from the shore. It was last used by the old Volunteers during World War I when the stones from a quarry there were shipped to build up the banks of the Caledonian Canal.

* * *

The village of Kessock is the nearest point on the Black Isle to Inverness. There have often been discussions about building a bridge at this estuary of the Beauly Firth, but putting aside the strong currents and tides there is the constant question of cost which overrules any such idea.

The *Eilean Dubh* ferry boat came into commission at the back end of 1951, and previously there had been a succession of ferry boats of varying degrees of efficiency, some built to carry vehicular traffic, others only for pedestrians.

The Kessock ferry certainly lessens the distance which many of the Black Islanders have to travel to Inverness. It takes time and petrol to go by road around the Firth.

Until the Second World War the ferry was privately owned, by the son of a former Inverness provost, who had the idea that a chain ferry was the only answer to the problem, and he set about to bring north his ideal. In fact, he tried three times, but disaster befell the lot.

The first sank at the Mull of Kintyre, and the second, procured from Penzance, sank on its voyage north, in the Bristol Channel. The third was a former Renfrew ferry boat on the Clyde, and it managed to reach Corpach, near Fort William, where it was found that the vessel was too wide to enter the Caledonian Canal. So alterations were made, but with little effect, and after a prolonged time the owners decided to take it round the Pentland Firth. Almost within sight of Kessock, at Tarbat Ness, it sank, and the chain ferry idea was abandoned.

Next a Dutch boat was purchased, actually twin boats joined together by a platform, and able to carry twenty cars. It was a splendid vessel—called the *Black Isle*—but was outsize for the pier and was later sold to the Government. The *Lowestoft Belle* chugged across the ferry during the war, but when it went out of commission, small passenger vessels replace it. These were the *Hope* and the *St. Mawes*, which carried on till the County Councils of Ross and Inverness took over the ferry.

The *Eilean Dubh* got its name from the Gaelic, meaning the Black Isle, suggested by a scholar in an Inverness school. The boat was specially built on Clydeside for the purpose.

There's a curious legend connected with Kessock about a young mermaid who was discovered on the shore by a man named Paterson. Attracted by this lovely stranger, he detained her and carefully pulled off her scale skin. Tradition tells us that by doing so, a mermaid loses her marine tendencies and becomes human.

The mermaid turned into a beautiful woman, and Paterson was so struck by her beauty that he took her home, and eventually married her.

Time went by, and they had several children, but nevertheless, the ex-mermaid never overcame a longing for the sea. She often besought her husband to give her back her scales, and promised that if he did so, he and his family would always be blessed with plenty of fish.

Many years passed and the family lived happily together until one of the children found the missing scales in an outshed and wondering what they were took them to his mother. When she saw them she grabbed them from the child and rushed down to the sea, where she was transformed into a mermaid, and was never seen again.

True to her promise, Kessock and the neighbouring villages are seldom without their fish, and Kessock herring are generally popular.

Apart from these small herring, even smaller fish, locally known as garvies, frequently came into the firth, and were caught in large numbers, packed in barrels and salted at Thornbush, Inverness.

They were then exported in bulk to Norway and shipped back to this country again as pilchards, or so is the belief in Kessock. These catches occurred about 20 years ago, but although garvies have been seen in Kessock waters more recently, few fishermen care to bother with such small fry.

There are still Patersons in Kessock, or rather at Craigton farther east, and they consist of several families of pilots, the main industry in the district.

Most of the coasters coming north to Inverness are traders in cement, coal and animal feeding stuffs, but until the beginning of the 20th century, small ships sailed up the Beauly Firth as far as Beauly.

In bygone days two competitive schools of pilots would race in rowing boats to meet incoming ships, but now the Patersons agree to work on friendlier terms!

20. SECOND SIGHT

I cannot pass Marybank without a visit to the Tower of Fairburn, at one time a stronghold of the MacKenzies of Seaforth, but now just a neglected ruin, beside the renovated buildings of a farm steading. Only the Tower and kitchen quarters remain, and the roof, made of oak shingles, was blown off practically in one piece at the time of the Peninsula War. The Tower was last occupied in 1770.

The present house of Fairburn is not old and was built in 1878 on the site of old Muirtown House (called after a place of the same name in the Black Isle). Earlier it was known as Wester Fairburn.

The Tower of Fairburn has many associations with the Brahan Seer's prophecies, and well known is the peculiar prophecy that a white cow would calve at the top of the Tower. At the time it seemed absurd, and practically impossible, but the incident actually did occur about a hundred years ago, when the farm was tenanted by a family of Chisholms, whose descendants still reside in the district.

The ruins of the Tower were then used as a two-storey barn, and on this particular day the corn harvest had been threshed, and the overflow of straw carried up a straight flight of stairs to the loft above, leaving a tell-tale trail behind. A white cow, heavy in calf, wandered into the barn through a large hole in the side of a wall, and following the straggling straw to the vaulted floor on the top storey she clambered up the stairs, and could not get down again. So there she calved, and the prophecy of the Brahan Seer came true.

Then again, the Seer said that when a tree growing up within the walls of the Tower became as thick as a cart wheel axle, the MacKenzies of Seaforth or their descendants would fall upon hard and disastrous times and there would be turmoil among the clans. So far no tree, in the literal sense, grows anywhere near the Tower, but a briar bush has taken root, which in the eyes of the Seer might easily be a tree.

A little less known is the interesting connection between the Tower of Fairburn and the Siege of Quebec, and the story was told to me by Mr Campbell at Marybank.

It is the tale of a young farm lad at Fairburn who stole some kebbocks of home-made cheese which the farmer's wife had carefully hidden in a sheaf of corn at the top of the Tower; but how the lad managed to scale the wall was a mystery nobody ever found out. Anyway, the culprit was caught, and paid the penalty of his theft by going to jail. On his release he not unnaturally felt the disgrace of his position, and joined a regiment of the Fraser Highlanders, who eventually took part in the siege of Quebec.

At the time the French troops were in possession of Quebec, and the Highlanders had been sent up to storm the battlements. But it seemed an impossibility to make an entry over the vast wall, until a Highland officer, one Simon Fraser, of the Balnain family, paraded his men and addressed them in Gaelic:

"C'ait am sheil an gillie dhirich tur Farabraon, agus a 'ghoid an caise?" (Where is the lad who climbed the Tower of Fairburn and stole the kebbock of cheese?)

Immediately the youth stepped forward and replied:

"Tha mi an so!" (I am here!).

Then the officer asked him if he would climb the wall.

So the lad took with him a thin rope attached at one end to a thicker piece, and successfully scaled the wall, pulled up the thick rope, and fixed it so that the other men could climb up too.

Not a word was spoken, but, "feeling a commotion," one French sentry called out:

"Qui vive!"

The Scots officer shouted back:

"La France!"

Alas! for the French, the sentry believed him, and presently the fort of Quebec was swarming with wild Highlanders, and the great city has ever since remained in the hands of the British.

Of interest, it may here be noted, the Siege of Quebec has been attributed to the Seaforth Highlanders, but this regiment was not raised until 18 years later, in 1778. According to my friend, Major C. I. Fraser of Reelig, the Highland regiment at Quebec was the Frasers' Highlanders (1757-63) No. 78 in the Army list, a number to which the Seaforths succeeded in 1778—hence the confusion!

The Church of Contin is among the oldest in the north, and along with the manse, glebe and steading, forms a unique holy island surrounded by the arms of Black Water River. It was founded in the 7th or 8th century by St. Maelrubha or Maolrubha, and was at one time a prebend of Fortrose Cathedral.

St. Maelrubha was of Irish lineage, and came to Scotland by way of Iona. He died of wounds he received from Norwegians who landed on the Black Isle on the 21st April, 722 A.D., and lies buried in Eilean Maree in Loch Maree, from whom the loch derives its name.

The Contin tokens still in use at Holy Communion bear the date 1786.

After the death of Sir Walter Scott, his amanuensis, William Laidlaw, became factor to MacKenzie of Seaforth, but his health gave way, and he came to reside with his brother, James, a sheep farmer in Contin. He died in 1845 at the age of 65 and was buried in Contin Churchyard.

Lochs abound in this area, the principal ones being at Achilty and Kinellan, and both boast an island. Strange to say these islands are artificial!

The isle in Loch Kinellan stands on logs of oak, and according to "Big Macleay," who possessed some property in the district, and would retire to this abode in hours of danger from his enemies. You can still see the remains of the buildings he occupied.

The isle in Loch Kenellan stands on logs of oak, and according to legend, was used also as a place of refuge, in this instance by the MacKenzies. About a quarter of a mile from the loch is Blar n'an Ceann—the field of heads—the scene of conflict between the MacKenzies and the MacDonells of Glengarry. The latter, after a great slaughter, were routed and were pursued by the MacKenzies as far as Moy, where the Black Water meets the Conon, and were forced into the water and drowned.

On the rising ground nearer Jamestown is the scene of another fierce battle, Blar na Pairc—"the Battle of the Park"—fought between the MacKenzies and the MacDonalds, in 1491. The cause of this battle appears to be the repudiation of Lady Margaret MacDonald by her husband, Kenneth MacKenzie, heir to the MacKenzie chieftainship, who sent her home in an insulting manner. The good lady had only one eye, and her husband mounted her on a one-eyed horse, and sent her off accompanied by a one-eyed man and a one eyed dog! In revenge, her cousin, Sir Alexander Mac-Donald of Lochalsh, invaded the MacKenzie country with a strong force of clansmen, but though a stronger army, were beaten back by the more able generalship of the MacKenzies.

*   *   *

Strathpeffer has rightly been labelled the Little City in the Hills! In summer it is the very hub of the Highlands, and daily bus loads of holidaymakers swarm into its friendly atmosphere from all quarters of the country. It is a great favourite with the tourists, though not so much an attraction in itself, but as a centre within easy reach of other beauty spots.

In pre-war days sufferers of rheumatism flocked to Strathpeffer to "take" the waters, and two special trains ran direct from London, such was the fame of this tiny Ross-shire hamlet. At the outbreak of war the army requisitioned the Pumproom, but it is now demolished and merely a memory of health-giving days. With the "spa," too, has gone the railway, and a year or two ago the existing track was uprooted and removed.

However, Strathpeffer has its other attractions. Home industries, tweed shops, and various Highland enterprises are fairly numerous. Tigh Mile Annas (The House of a Thousand Wonders) helps to boost local handicrafts, including staghorn buttons and brooches made in the village by an ex-navy serviceman.

The Pavilion is a popular rendezvous for the visitor, with its tearoom and dance hall. Local clubs organise dances, and invite well-known bands from the south to make their music; and some of the best Scottish dance bands pay repeated visits to these and other Strathpeffer dances.

The Strathpeffer Highland Games were started in 1882, and have been continued annually, except during the two wars, and oddly enough in the years 1933-5, when there seemed to be a great scarcity of horses in the north, and equine sports were abandoned.

Formerly the Games were a two-day event, with horse racing on the Friday, and other sports on the Saturday. Steeple-chasing preceeded flat racing at the "Strath," held in the two fields opposite the main gates to Castle Leod, home of Lord and Lady Tarbat, but in later years the field beside the Castle has been in regular use.

The road to Auchterneed branches off the main Dingwall road between Strathpeffer and Fodderty, and of interest to the antiquary is a Cup-Marked Stone; but I have not been able to find out much of its significance. It is generally believed to have something to do with divination. On its surface are about a dozen cup-marks.

Also in the vicinity is the Raven's Rock, where you can hear a remarkable echo.

Castle Leod, the home of Lord and Lady Tarbat, is said to have been built by Sir Roderick MacKenzie, tutor of Kintail, in 1616, and was one of the seats of the Earl of Cromarty. Built of red sandstone, it has a fine baronial appearance.

A connection with the Brahan Seer comes to light with the "Eagle Stone"—*Clach an Tiompain*—patterned with a horse-shoe shape above an eagle. It was of this stone that the seer prophesied that "the day will come when ships will ride, their cables attached to *Clach an Tiompain*."

Tradition recalls that the stone marks the spot of another clan fray between the MacKenzies of Seaforth and the Munroes. The story tells that at the time the Lady of Seaforth, who dwelt in a wicker house at Kinellan, was kidnapped along with all her belongings by a party of Munroes. The MacKenzies overtook the party near Castle Leod, and there was teriffic slaughter, causing many casualties among the Munroes; and I am told that the Eagle Stone was set up by the vanquished clan in memory of their fallen comrades.

Before we leave this wonderful countryside, I must refer for a moment to magnificent Ben Wyvis, overshadowing the valley of Strathpeffer. Rising 3,426 feet above sea level, its top is covered with a soft green sward. The principal proprietor holds the right of its possession on condition that he can present to the Crown a snowball from its height at any time of the year! I believe the old ben is never without snow, even in the hottest summer.

The name of Fodderty is supposed to be derived from two Gaelic words—*fo* and *ràth*—signifying "a meadow along the side of a hill," as indeed is the parish.

On the south side of the valley is Knockfarrel Hill (693 ft.) with "the hill of the high stone place or house" as its derivation, and it owes its name to the site of a vitrified fort, one of the finest specimens in the north. The ruins are scattered over an acre surrounding a plain, and the fort was probably built as a means of protection against invading enemies. The stones have been cemented together by fire, as the buildings were erected long before the discovery of lime.

I wonder how many folk who live in and around Dingwall have noticed the town's old Tower, standing in the centre of the municipal Buildings! The Town Clock pedestalled on a grey wooden erection surmounting the Tower has a familiar face which every Dingwallian knows, but I gather from many of them that they have never seen the Tower! I doubt whether those who know of its existence have bothered to find out anything about it! It is all that remains of the old Tolbooth, built in 1730, and at the west end of the Council Buildings stand the Old Mercat Cross. Beside it a grating can be seen, and history records that it formerly guarded the window of the murderer's cell at the foot of the Tower.

Sir Hector MacDonald's Monument stands prominently on Mitchell Hill, the latter gifted to the town by a former councillor of that name. From the monument, by the way, you can see yet another memorial tower at Millbuie on the Black Isle, the place of Sir Hector's birth.

Before joining the army Sir Hector MacDonald served his apprenticeship as a draper in Dingwall, the town which later feted him and prepared a banquet in his honour after he became hero of Omdurman. There is a great deal of mystery about his death, and he is supposed to have committed suicide in France. His remains were brought back to Scotland in a sealed coffin, which not even his brother was allowed to open, and buried in the Dean Cemetery, Edinburgh, beneath a heavy concrete slab. Some repudiated this idea of his death and believed that he would appear once again as a hero on a great occasion.

Eastwards, the Cromarty Firth stretches far beyond the town, and, hidden among the trees, Dingwall's old Castle.

It was the principal fortress of the Earldom of Ross, and associated with it were several earls, including Finlaec, the father of MacBeth, immortalised by Shakespeare. When peace came to the Highlands after the Norse Invasion danger passed, the castle fell into ruin, and was later turned into a quarry from which many of the town's present buildings have been built. Only the entrance of one of the main towers, traces of the moat, and part of the flanking towers are the surviving remnants of Dingwall's Castle to-day.

Peculiar to Dingwall are the number of churches and banks in the town. Seven of each. The pre-Reformation Church of Dingwall was accidentally burned by a citizen shooting pigeons. His charge set fire to the thatch! The present building included in its structure an old Pictish Stone, which stands now at the churchyard gate.

Having taken a "bird's eye-view" of the town, we descended the steep Tower stairs to the Council Chambers, where we examined two magnificent swords presented to Sir Hector MacDonald and displayed in a glass cabinet beneath a fine portrait of the great soldier. One of these, a present from the Donald Society, has a silver scabbard beautifully ornamented with badges in 18-carat gold, with a hilt of similar value. The blade was tempered in Italy.

In another glass case I examined caskets presented to Sir Hector when he received the Freedom of the Burgh. On the opposite wall hangs a copy of a "Titian," once believed to be an original, and worth £30,000!

The Council Buildings link up with Dingwall's Carnegie Hall, built in 1903, and added to later, being re-opened in 1926, to commemorate the sept-centenary of the gifting of the Royal Charter to Dingwall in 1226 by Alexander II. It is one of the best halls in the North of Scotland, with seating capacity to accommodate a thousand folk.

21. THE BLACK ISLE

One of the sweetest lodges I know stands on the Great North Road at the entrance to Highfield House, just north of Muir of Ord. It reminds me of a sentinel at the gateway to fairyland, as this quaint little cottage is designed in hobgoblin fashion.

Alas! if you pass through the iron gateway, the rough stoney road no longer leads to some fine mansion house, and your journey ends in a scene of pitiful ruin. Only rubble now remains of one of the recognised "seats" of a branch of the MacKenzies of Seaforth.

The original house was bought by George Gillanders in 1781 from his cousin, MacKenzie of Applecross, and later the two families were to be united in marriage. Gillanders was an Aberdeenshire man, and held the position of commissioner or factor to the Lord Seaforth of that day, in Lewis.

The original house, once occupied by the Bishops of Ross, was burned all but the west wing in 1871, and rebuilt seven years later; but the final fire which occurred a few years ago is believed to have started in the original wing.

Farther along the north road from Highfield we come to another lodge, at the entrance to Conan House, which, I understand, was bought by the MacKenzies of Gairloch as a home, to be nearer Inverness than their west coast estate.

As a boy of sixteen, Hugh Miller, the famous author and geologist, lived nearby with his uncle, a mason, and helped in the building of Conan House and farm steading. In fact, the farm grieve told me that there are several stones on the steading building inscribed with Hugh Miller's initials.

Close by Conan House is an old burying ground, still in use, which is consecrated to St. Bride, and the site of a pre-Reformation chapel, also dedicated to St. Bride, though no trace of the latter can now be seen. Other references to St. Bride crop up in local names, and in 1481 a bloody battle is supposed to have taken place at a nearby ford between the MacDonalds of the Isles and the armies of James III. The battle is known as Lagabread, derived from the Gaelic, *"Lagaidh-Bride."* At this ford Hugh Miller once had a narrow escape from drowning.

Balavil House lies across the road from the Conan estate, but I can find no information about it except that it is simply the dower house of Conan. However, within a short distance of Balavil is David's Fort, believed to be the site of a battle in the days of Scottish kings, but may have been used later as a watch tower to guard the ford at Conan.

I often think of Conon-Bridge as one of the more picturesque villages in Scotland. As you come into the village from the south, your eye is at once attracted by a small wooden porch pillared on either side with an inscribed tablet; one written in English; the other in Gaelic. Within the grounds are the Nurses' Homes of Ross and Cromarty, erected to the memory of Sir Kenneth Smith MacKenzie of Gairloch, former Lord Lieutenant of the County, by his fellow-countrymen as a token of respect for his long public services.

In former days a brick factory offered employment locally, besides a meal mill at Ussie Mills.

Standing on a hill overlooking the village is the Seaforth Sanatorium which was erected before the 1914-18 war by Lady Seaforth for tuberculosis patients. Then during that war it was taken over for Belgian patients, and later for sick children. During the second war, it became a military hospital, and now once again the walls echo with children's voices.

The name Ussie brings to mind the famous Brahan Seer, Kenneth MacKenzie, who lived near Loch Ussie, where his prophetic stone is claimed to lie. Coinneach was a Lewis man who came over to this area with the Lords of Seaforth.

Brahan Castle, the stronghold of the MacKenzies of Seaforth, has recently been practically dismantled, and only the walls remain standing.

Near Maryburgh are evidences of Druid stones, which appear to be the remains of a chambered cairn, and only 60 yards from the roadside you may find in Brahan Wood three large conglomerate stones, which were once "consulted for responses."

As East Lothian has been christened "The Garden of Scotland," I think we could claim the Black Isle as the Garden of the North. Of course, some folk will disagree with me—especially those from Easter Ross (which sometimes claims the title), but I am told there is no better stretch of land for growing barley, at any rate, than that area between Conon-Bridge and Findon.

The parish of Urquhart and Wester Logie is a wide one embracing such villages as Culbokie, Alcaig and Conon-Bridge, and stretches a distance of ten miles from the boundaries of Urray on the west to Resolis on the east. It is fine and open, commanding a splendid view of the Cromarty Firth, and indeed the thought of the sun beating down on the old ruins of an ancient kirk by the sea-shore still lingers in my memory.

Tradition relates that the place name, Urquhart, is derived from a lady of that name, who built the first church in the parish. She was

Sophia Urquhart, of the family of Cromarty, and had been allotted the lands in her dowry. But according to Watson's *Place Names of Ross and Cromarty,* the author states the name comes from the Welsh and means "among the woodlands." Logie is derived from the Gaelic and means "a hollow," and is descriptive of another old church on the south bank of the River Conon. It is now called Logie Wester to distinguish it from a parish of that name in the Synod, and forms the west division of the united parish.

Perhaps Ferintosh is the best known district of the parish, which has been closely associated with the family of Forbes of Culloden, the present representative of them living in Ryefield House.

The derivation of Ferintosh is also from the Gaelic—*"Fearann an Tois'eachd"*—meaning "the land of the Chief or Thane." In 1430 it became part of the Thanage of Cawdor, and until 1889 was included in the county of Nairn.

Between 1690 and 1785 you could brew your own whisky without fear of the local excisemen, as during this period Ferintosh was the only privileged area allowed to practise home distilling. The reason dates back to the 1688 Revolution, when the privilege was granted to Forbes of Culloden in recognition of services rendered to the King in repayment of outlays on behalf of the Government, and also to recompense him for the destruction of his property at Ferintosh by the Government soldiers who ravaged all his distilleries.

The district enjoyed these privileges for over 90 years until this right was bought back by the Government in 1785.

I am told other kinds of spirits now haunt Ferintosh, and a decided association in the village of Culbokie in its name—"nook of the hobgoblins"; and on Findon burn there's a small gorge once believed to be the abode of a *"bean shith"*—a lady fairy.

I am also told that the last murderer to be hanged in Inverness committed his crime in Ferintosh, and of interest too, are the derivations of two local places—Balnabeen, "the place of trial," and Crochar, "the hanging place."

The village of Jemimaville, named after a lady of the family of Munro of Ardoch, is one-sided; but the villagers have to cross the road to fetch their water. For years it was most dangerous to attempt this crossing to the outside pumps with cars swooping upon them at speed, and after much protestations, the local committee for village affairs persuaded the County Council to declare theirs a "built-up area" and grant them the thirty-mile limit after street lighting had been installed.

Although the village name is Jemimaville, its post office is Poyntzfield, and steals the tag from the Poyntzfield estate. The latter was formerly Ardoch, but owing to the marriage of one of the

Munroes, to a Miss Poyntz, an English heiress, the name was changed in her honour at about the beginning of the eighteenth century.

* * *

You might almost dare to call Cromarty a "dead" town, yet it still has an attraction for visitors who regularly come back every summer for their holidays. All the usual recreations are enjoyed by the younger folk, and one of the highlights of the season is the regatta, including various aquatic sports.

The rope factory provided work for about 250 local people, while another 600 women were employed spinning yarn throughout Ross-shire. But the introduction of power machinery in the weaving trade was too strong an opposition for a burgh that lacked the essentials for such a working plant.

Of course, Cromarty is an old fishing port, and in 1897 the fishing fleet numbered sixty-six vessels. To-day's total—none! How the times have changed! In these days crews were gathered from men in Avoch, now reputed to be the richest little fishing port in Scotland. The women were the hardest workers, not only baiting the lines, but carrying their menfolk out to the boats on their backs and bringing home the catches in baskets from the boats to the shore. Little wonder the rising generation of girls decided to seek employment elsewhere, which was probably the cause of the Cromarty fishing fate. The population was more than double the size it is to-day.

Sailing vessels also made Cromarty a departure port for America, and the Allan Line was the company trading on this route.

Like all fishing villages family names have stayed, and commonest among them are the Hoggs, Skinners, Watsons and Hossacks. Confusion in identity was inevitable, so it is not unnatural that we find nicknames, some hereditary, which are in everyday use. For instance, there's big Lobster Bob; Stichy and Tommy Yankee. They are known by no other name. Even in the church records the nicknames are written in brackets after the proper ones.

Perhaps the two most famous sons of Cromarty were Hugh Miller, and Sir Thomas Urquhart, the translator of Rabelais. Sir Thomas was born in 1613, and died on the continent after an eventful life. Nearly a hundred of his literary manuscripts were lost when he was taken prisoner at the Battle of Worcester in 1651, and for a time he was later confined in the Tower of London, where, to convince Cromwell of his own importance, he wrote his *True Pedigree of the Urquhart Family,* in which he traced his ancestry back to Adam. He escaped to France and died there in a fit of laughter on learning of the restoration of Charles II. He is buried in Cullicudden.

However, I rather feel that people are inclined to forget Sir Thomas Urquhart, who is overshadowed by the fame of a more recent figure in literature, Hugh Miller, whose best known work is undoubtedly *My Schools and Schoolmasters*. I am afraid most of his writing is pretty heavy going, though he gives some interesting accounts of local doings of his day, and lore of the countryside.

His birthplace is the only preserved thatched cottage in Cromarty, and is open at certain times of the day for inspection. In October 1952 the town commemorated the 150th anniversary of his birth.

The first time I visited Cromarty I had considerable difficulty in finding the white-washed cottage, though it was unmistakably unique when it eventually appeared into view! I found myself doing an unrehearsed tour of the town before finally getting there, having asked numerous residents for "Hugh Miller's House" as if he was the local grocer in the town! I had every sympathy for the little lad who was asked by a lady on the 150th anniversary day why he wasn't at school and replied:

"Oh, Hugh Miller's dead!"

The cottage has four rooms, and of special interest is the room where Hugh Miller was born. In it are preserved some of his every-day treasures—his mallet; his plaid; the desk at which he worked as agent in the Commercial Bank; and old copies of the *Witness*, an Edinburgh paper he edited. In an adjoining room, glass cases contain many of his geological specimens, and letters he received from famous characters of his day, such as Thomas Carlyle, Charles Darwin, and Rev. Dr. Chalmers. I also saw a copy of a letter from Queen Victoria granting a pension to his widow. A sundial in the garden is one of Miller's earliest carvings, which he had designed and cut to prove to his uncles, who had brought him up, that "he was above average in the art of hewing."

Hugh Miller's father was an old navy man, who perished at sea in a storm when his son was a mere boy of five.

*   *   *

On Gallow Hill, behind the town of Cromarty, men were hung for small offences such as sheep-stealing, and on the road leading in this direction I found the old churchyard of St. Regulus, now chained and padlocked to forbid entrance. The oldest stone, I am told, bears the figure of a claymore and is dated 1600.

Across the road from St. Regulus' Churchyard is the entrance to the Cromarty House tunnel, which echoes not a very nice memory of former days. To-day the iron gate is closed and locked, but the present laird's ancestors used the tunnel as a servant's entrance, so that they would not be seen by members of the family! Many a time the poor of the town haunted the back doors to beg bread from the kitchens, and later the message boys delivering goods from the town stores trod their way through it to the back premises. What mockery! The modern butcher and baker drive up in style in his polished van and nobody thinks anything of it!

22.   THREADS OF HISTORY

There seems little doubt of the fact that the area now known as the Black Isle was once an island, but how it came by this name is a matter of opinion. It certainly lies in a belt of temperate climate and one theory is that in really wintry weather the Black Isle only takes on a mild sprinkling of snow or even none at all. Again, some say it derived its name from the great amount of forestry on it. My friend, the late John N. MacLeod, a noted Gaelic authority, maintains it is called after the patron saint of Rosemarkie, St. Duthac (Gaelic *Dubhthach*), who similarly lends his name to Loch Duich in Wester Ross, which I believe is more probable, with the Gealic form, *Eilean Dubh*. The old name, he told me, was *Ardmeanach*—the middle height.

It is a prosperous peninsula, containing splendid agricultural land, and many of its farms are among the best known in the north. On the whole it is a very dry area, and the natives rely mostly on wells and spring water for drinking supplies, although several schemes are afoot to make a new source in a loch on the Alness side of the Cromarty Firth.

The road from Muir of Ord to Cromarty is classed as the only "A" road, and connects the larger places on the Black Isle, such as Munlochy, Avoch, Fortrose, and Rosemarkie, and the latter two burghs are favourite holiday resorts for summer visitors. Even tiny Tore has its hotel, and it is easy to wonder what is the attraction with such an isolated community. Primarily, it is central, at a road junction from both Muir of Ord and Conon-Bridge, and farther east to Kessock or Fortrose.

The name Tore is derived from the Gaelic—*an Todhar*, "the bleaching spot"—but another derivation appears to be "hungry hill," owing to the poverty of the pasture, and it was noted in the past for its horse markets. Memories of "bloody warfare" are still recalled by some of the natives, who tell me the place used to "run with blood" with tinker's squabbles after the Wool Fair in Inverness!

Lying between the two thoroughfares to Conon-Bridge and Muir of Ord is the 17th century Kilcoy Castle, and for many years it was practically a ruin and roofless. It was re-roofed about ninety years ago, and is habitable once again, though only in charge of a caretaker. It was built on the site of old Pictish remains, and within a short distance are some of the best existing Druid Circles in the Highlands. They date back to the third century. I have been told of the ghost too, or, at least, the haunted room.

It is curious to find traces of Episcopacy in a Highland country parish, but the church at Arpafeelie still hangs together, even with a small congregation of twenty members. No longer is a rector resident, but the charge is shared by two itinerants from Glenurquhart and Dingwall. I was interested to see the old Church register containing births, marriages and deaths from 1785-1835, and was particularly intrigued with the custom of christening new-born babes, two or three days after birth. In several instances the same man's name appears as parent for various births in the parish!

In the Warren, among a shroud of beech trees, are the remains of a Druid Circle, and although very much overgrown you can still see the general layout and the altar stone. One hollowed specimen is said to be a sacrificial stone, and the story goes that long ago farmers used it as a water trough for their cattle; and all caught some dreadful disease and died.

In 1340 the MacDonalds and the people of Inverness fought a battle in this district—the Battle of Blar na Coi. Their chief weapon appears to have been an ordinary plough yoke—hence the derivation of the name—"battle of the yoke." History relates that of the beaten party only one man survived, and he took refuge under an over-turned *carnloban*, a kind of farm cart. As a result he was nicknamed "Loban," and so we find the origin of a north country name with the other form of "Logan."

Close by is the farm and hill of Drumderfit, with the associated derivation, "the ridge of tears." It was formerly Drumdubh—"the black ridge," but as the Gaelic folk were wont to say:

Bu druim dubh an dé thu, ach is druima diar an diugh thu."
(Black ridge wert thou yesterday, but ridge of tears to-day).

*   *   *

Sheltered at the head of Munlochy Bay is a village of melody, as until quite recently Munlochy boasted at least three choirs, all of them regular competitors in the annual Ross-shire Musical Festival. The church choir is a limb of the kirk, and the Educational Authority Continuation Choir was formed from one of the singing continuation classes, while the third choir is representative of some of the lady members of this choir.

Due south of Munlochy on the westermost headland of Munlochy Bay is the hill of Craigiehowe, which legend associates with the hero, Finn. His cave on the water's edge is supposed to extend to Loch Lundy, almost a mile and a half away, and in the old days, water dripping from a well in the roof was said to be a cure for deafness.

A roadside well, before the traveller reaches the Munlochy loop road end, appears to have little significance apart from being a lucky "clooty" well, with the adjacent wire fence gaily adorned with every colour of cloth; but the holy well—"*Tobar Creagag*"—near Bennetsfield, above Munlochy Bay, is still visited on the first Sunday of May, and offerings thrown into it for luck.

About half-way between Munlochy and Avoch on the east side of Munlochy Bay on Ormond Hill (or, as it is sometimes called, Ladyhill) are the foundations of Ormond Castle, where the first banner of Scottish Independence was raised in the time of Robert the Bruce. The castle was built of red sandstone, and some of the stones were removed to help in the building of the present Inverness Castle. Only a few trees, the residue of a belt of woodland, are left as a landmark for boats coming up the firth, and help to identify the actual position of the castle.

Rosehaugh House, almost hidden from the road by trees, represents a mixture of Elizabethan and French architecture, and was built in the later part of the last century by the late James Douglas Fletcher, reputed to be among the wealthiest proprietors in the Highlands.

Memories of the past still haunt the steading of Rosehaugh Mains, once the home of a famous strain of Shorthorn cattle. Horses, too, figured prominently on this 212-acre farm, and once a hundred horses and ponies were stabled in the premises, while a private racecourse stretched in length for three-quarters of a mile. An immense silo, excavated from the side of a hill, is yet another relic of many years ago.

* * *

Ninety per cent of the 2,000 villagers of Avoch belong to the families of Patience, MacLeman and Jack, and about 300 of that number have the name of Patience. Little wonder there is some confusion, and to counteract that, by-names are legion.

The "Avochiedolies," as the natives are generally called, are unique in having a dialect of their own, not unlike the Buchan accent, used only among themselves. It takes a quick ear on the part of the visitor to understand this strange tongue, so it is really seldom spoken outside the village.

Perhaps the reason for these distinctive families and this dialect lies in the fact that Avoch was always a fishing village, and the family fishing businesses have been handed down through the generations. The men-folk knew no other life.

Long before the railway came to the Black Isle a steamer sailed between Inverness and Fortrose, but was not able to call at Avoch due to the shallowness of the water there. But Avoch was not forgotten for all that, and still remembered is Big Kate Allison, who regularly met the steamer with her skiftie and rowed her passengers to the shore. Many a time she carried them to safety when her skiftie got stranded in shallow water, and once it capsized with the loss of fourteen lives.

There's plenty of "go" in the people of Avoch, and typical of their public spirit are the amenities of the village. It all began several years ago when a few local enthusiasts decided to collect enough money to build a pleasure ground. They held the usual whist drives and concerts during the winter, and in the summer gala weeks helped to swell the funds until, with the help of a Government grant, the magnificent sum of £6,000 was collected.

Now they have a bowling green, tennis courts, curling pond, playground for the kiddies, and a pavilion with a dual purpose of clubhouse and hall. A football pitch is the most recent innovation, with natural terracing on the face of a hill for the spectators. Avoch folk have always been good footballers, and long ago two teams were made up of Patiences and Jacks.

I like Avoch (pronounced "a'ach"). It's such a typical little fishing village, with its sheltered harbour, and the fishermen's nets drying on every available nearby fence.

Avoch House was burnt in 1820, and its empty shell is still called the "Burnt House" by local folk. For many years it was the home of Sir Alex. MacKenzie, the famous pioneer, after whom the Mac-Kenzie River in Canada was called.

The cathedral dates back to 1330 A.D., and older still is the chapter house, now a Freemasons' lodge. Until the Reformation the chapter house was thatched, and the cathedral roof made of lead, but history records that James VI ordered the roof to be removed to add to the wealth of the country's treasury. Before the First World War the building was taken over by the Ministry of Works and grouted.

At this time the original foundations were found to be covered with a wonderful collection of mason's marks, now believed to be the finest in the country.

Fortrose and Rosemarkie were annexed in 1455 by James II, to form the Burgh of Fortrose, and although both places retain a certain amount of individualism, a firm bond lies between them. In 1590 James IV made Fortrose a Royal Burgh, and two years later ratified the charter granted by James II. In 1612 he confirmed the charters of both burghs and united them anew under the Provost, Bailies and Council of Fortrose.

The town takes its name from Fort Ross, an ancient stronghold of the MacKenzies of Seaforth, but although the actual building is no longer in existence, you will still find evidence of it in the names of a yard and street at the east end of the burgh. The former name of Chanonry—Gaelic, *"A' Chananaich,"* meaning Canonry—is still given to a point jutting out into the Moray Firth, almost opposite Fort George, where the Brahan Seer is reputed to have been burnt at the stake, having foretold the downfall of the MacKenzies of Seaforth.

Until about thirty years ago salmon fishing was the main industry in both Fortrose and Rosemarkie, and in those days salmon could be bought for threepence per pound. Even farm workers made a clause in their feeing contracts that they would not be fed on salmon more than twice in the week!

But since a fishing syndicate decided to alter the limits of the firth estuary, only sweep nets are permitted. The object, it seemed, was to let more salmon go up the rivers and fill the rich man's larder, and not unnaturally it caused a lot of ill feeling in the district.

In Rosemarkie the salmon fishers collected ice in winter from ponds in the Fairy Glen, which aided preservation in packing the fish; and in frosty weather the crofters helped by carting the ice blocks down to the ice house at Chanonry Point. Remnants of old kilns recall pre-railway days when salmon were smoked before being dispatched by boat to southern markets.

One of the few relics of interest in Rosemarkie is a Celtic stone, with the Pictish symbols of spectacles and a mirror, and the usual Celtic sculpture. It was found in 1735, along with some stone coffins, in a vault under the floor of the Parish Church, standing on the site of the original church dedicated to St. Boniface. In fact, it may have rested on his grave.

23. HIGHWAYMEN

Beaufort Castle, the home of Lord Lovat, Chief of the Clan Fraser, is the thirteenth building on that site, and the present castle was built in 1882. It stands on the site of Beaufort or Downie, which was mentioned in early history as far back as the era of Alexander I, when still visible trenches were dug. It was seized by Oliver Cromwell and the citadel blown up, and immediately after Culloden was burnt to the ground by the Duke of Cumberland's Army. The flames were witnessed by Simon, Lord Lovat, from a mountain near Loch Muilie, in Glenstrathfarrar, where he and a few of his faithful followers had retreated.

Before the Frasers came into possession of the Lovat estate it belonged to the Bissets, and the Frasers appear to have come into Inverness-shire about the end of the thirteenth century from Peebles and Tweeddale.

The Lovat Shinty team was formed about 1886, and most of the active male members of the community have played in the team at some stage of their careers. Numerous Kiltarlity families have been connected with it throughout the years, and apart from the Thows, I might mention the Campbells, MacKenzies, Livingstones, Rosses and Macraes. The late Lord Lovat and his brother, Major Hugh Fraser, were both playing members. Also among the team were Theodore Campbell and Donald Ross, both noted athletes of their day. The late Major Dewar, for many years the estate factor, who died in 1951, was the last surviving member of the team.

In the early days the chief opponents were Strathglass and Glenurquhart, and Lovat gave a very good account of themselves. In 1906 they won their first big success — the MacTavish Cup — and have since won nearly all the major trophies many times.

The name Tomnacross is derived from the Gaelic — *Tom-na-croiche* — "hill of the scaffold", and on the hill concerned the parish church was built in 1800, after the old Kiltarlity Church, near the Black Bridge, fell into disrepair. It was built adjoining the hangman's noose. A mound beside it was once a Baron Baillie's Court, held by officials of the estate, which had strict codes of law of its own. It was introduced as part of the Feudal system, and dealt with such offences as murder, theft, poaching, bad behaviour and breaches of the estate rules.

In 1925 an old oak tree on the east side of the mound, which, according to tradition, was the original hanging tree, was cut down to provide lairs for a certain family.

There is much evidence of Druid stones and circles in Kiltarlity parish, and down from the church on Tomnacross Farm are the remains of a stone circle. Across the road on the Lovat estate are two joined stone circles.

Other Druid stones are to be seen at Culburnie, and a "punch hole" is well-preserved near Bruiach Farm.

Incidentally, Bruicheach Island is artificial and built on vitrified rock with a base of oak pillars. A number of years ago a monk from Fort Augustus descended in a diving suit and brought to the surface a piece of oak wood as a souvenir.

Meal mills were once numerous, too, and the one at Bruiach was equipped with some of the finest machinery in the Highlands. Fire destroyed the lot. I have failed to trace the original date of the Bruiach Meal Mill, but, I believe, it was at least two hundred years old. James Livingstone, who stays nearby, once told me that the uncovered an old tombstone in Tomnacross Kirkyard, which stated that it had been put there by Hugh Chisholm, miller at Bruiach, 1756.

Leaving Tomnacross and taking the hill road to Loch Ness, the road begins a steady climb, until it descends again into Glen Convinth. I have not found anything of historical interest in the glen except, perhaps, the ruins of an old church, which dates back to the beginning of the 13th century. It was originally a small monastery. The churchyard is still used by local families, including the folk from Abriachan, a few miles away.

Until fifteen to twenty years ago, when cars in the Highlands were more the exception than the rule, funeral hearses and waggonettes were drawn by horses. On cold wintry days when funerals came over to Glen Convinth the horses found food and stabling at Convinth farm, while the farmer's wife provided warmth and nourishment for the shivering drivers.

There have been generations of MacKenzies at Convinth farm, but the last of them died in 1947, and now the farm is run as a dairy by a Caithness man. Mrs Annie MacKenzie, widow of the previous tenant, still lives at Convinth Croft, and she was able to give me a picture of present day life in the glen, telling me that in spite of their distance from apparent civilisation, the folk in the glen were by no means isolated.

The incident occured at the beginning of the eighteenth century, when farmers paid their workers either annually or bi-annually. The farmer in question hailed from Glenurquhart, and one day, near the end of the harvest, he called for a volunteer amongst his men to ride over to Inverness, via Glen Convinth, to collect the harvest wages from the bank. But knowing the reputation of the Bunchrew highwayman who waylaid unsuspecting travellers along the quiet road between Beauly and Inverness, not even the toughest worker would agree to undertake the mission.

Just when the farmer was at his wits end to know what to do, Daft Davie, the orra lad on the farm, offered his services, but thinking such a suggestion was too ridiculous, the farmer turned down the lad's offer.

But Davie protested that he could hoodwink the bandit, and at last persuaded his master to give him a trial.

"Go in to the stable and take the pick of my horses," said the master, "because you will need all the speed you can get to outrun the thief."

So Davie thanked him and promised he would do his best.

Next morning the farmer rose to find that Davie had already left, and going into his stable he discovered to his horror that all his fine steeds were still in their stalls, and Davie had selected the most aged and broken down old mare he could find.

"The foolish fellow. He can never expect to get away with that," he raged.

However, by this time Davie was well on his way, and jogging along at a slow trot without a care in the world. He was now miles from home and had passed his half-way mark when out of a wood came a stranger on horseback, and by his apparel Davie decided that there indeed was the great man himself who was scaring the life out of all travellers on the highway. Davie was quite unperturbed, and as the horseman accompanied him along the road, he was quite glad of his companionship, and readily answered all his questions about where he was going and what was his mission.

Davie had no secrets. He told the fellow he was travelling to Inverness to collect his master's money to pay the harvest workers, and he even gave him an idea as to the value of the purse. No, he wasn't afraid of robbers by the roadside.

After a mile or two the stranger departed, and once again disappeared into the shadows from which he had come.

Davie reached Inverness without any further hitch, and with little difficulty contacted the tradesman who in those days acted as banker, and was given in charge of the purse. But before leaving he asked for an identical dummy package, which he wanted sealed and stitched similar to the real one. Having got what he required he set off for home.

At Bunchrew his fellow traveller from the inward journey was waiting for him, but Davie showed no sign of fear, and hailed him as a friend.

"Did you get the money?" the stranger grunted.

Davie nodded.

"Then hand it over to me."

"I cannot do that," replied Davie. "It's my master's money, and if he finds out that I lost it, he will dismiss me."

The stranger produced his pistol.

"Are you going to give me the money?" he demanded angrily, and as Davie felt in his pocket for his purse, a wry smile was on the highwayman's face.

"That's better. Give it to me," he said.

"I'll not hand it to you," replied Davie, and threw the dummy packet on to the roadside. Then turning his old nag he continued on his way, until he was out of sight round the next corner.

The highwayman snatched the purse from the ground, and drawing his fine steed into the shelter of a wood, began to untie the stitchings and break the seals. So intent was he on his prize that he did not notice the brave Davie creep up alongside his horse, mount it, and before the robber could stop them, horse and man were gone, and he was left with an old done mare!

There is a sequel to this true story, which occurred two years later. Davie by chance was drinking in an inn, when he heard voices in the adjoining room, through the thin bar partition, which made him put down his glass and listen.

"And how was it you came to lose all your money?" one man was asking.

"That was due to the loss of my horse," replied the other. "It was stolen from me two years ago, and I kept all my fortune sewn up in my saddle. When the horse went, so did the money." The speaker was the highwayman.

On hearing this piece of news, Davie could not wait to finish his drink, and without letting himself be recognised he was off home as quickly as possible to tell his master. A search was made for the saddle, long since thrown on the rubbish heap, but at last it was found, and the leather split open. The highwayman was as good as his word, for hidden in his saddle was money valued at over a thousand pounds!

As might almost be expected in a peaceful glen like Convinth, there was much smuggling done in the past, and few folk were without their own stills for making "the wheesky." It is only a few years since "The Swapper" (a nickname given to a local horse and dog dealer) died, and he was reputed to be the last known surviving smuggler in the district. He dug his own bothy on the hillside where he successfully brewed his special brand for years, and it was only discovered when gamekeepers were burning the heather and accidentally came across the bothy, complete with full working plant and barrels.

Many a time the 'keepers were on "The Swapper's" trail, as it was not only the whisky he brewed illegally, but he was wont to poach grouse, and easily found his own market for them. Between 'keepers and excisemen he was often on the run!

24.   LANDS FROM THE SEA

I have every sympathy with the motorist visitor to Inverness who enters the town from the east or the south. Barracks, distilleries, railway sidings and livestock auction markets bound his path, and presently he is lost in the narrow one-way streets of the Highland Capital. But once the outer shell of traffic congestion is pierced, there is warmth in the welcome which the Highlander can provide.

It is an unfortunate approach to this great county town, but one which may be rectified if planners' blue-prints ever materialise. We may yet see a wider and more suitable entrance to the centre of the Scottish Highlands.

However, this book does not directly concern the Capital itself, but the districts so easily reached from Inverness to the east and to the south. We leave the town the way we enter, along Millburn Road to the junction of the Aberdeen and Perth highways.

Taking the former, we presently find ourselves in sight of the Moray Firth, bordered on the far shore by the Black Isle and Easter Ross.

Stoneyfield House nearby is run as a guest-house and away back in history is believed to have been used by the monks of Elgin Cathedral, and in more recent times was tenanted by Mrs Gordon Cumming for forty years.

Nearby is Ashton Farm where a couple of rather remarkable stones, probably marriage stones, have been built into the farmhouse garden wall. Dated 1669 and surmounted by a thistle and a rose, they were dug up by a farmer when he was ploughing a field.

Stratton Lodge was built as a dower house for Culloden in the 1770's, and another wing was added to it in 1930.

A Miss Stratton, a very wealthy lady, gave her name to the house," said Lieut-General Sir Kenneth MacLeod, the late owner, "and incidentally Stratton Street in London is called after the same lady."

An "S" bend under the railway bridge at this main Nairn Road, beside the entrance gate to Stratton Lodge, is well-known to the motorist, but by avoiding it and taking the rough track along the firthside we come to Milton Farm, now split up into holdings. The farmhouse, I am told, was in earlier times an inn. However, one story tells of an underground tunnel leading under the house, which was used by smugglers arriving by boat to deliver their illicit liquor at the inn.

I am inclined to dub Allanfearn "the place of the yellow sheep", due to the dye or dip favoured by the farmer. Within the farm boundaries are a few fine specimens of Druid Circles in excellent preservation, and these can be seen from the roadside.

At Allanfearn I crossed the railway on the left and made my way towards Alturlie. I arrived at the Point and the little village I found nestling alone on the water's edge. No natives now remain in the long row of thatched and slate-roofed cottages.

Along the shore, only accessible by footpath, is Clattach, so near sea-level that high tides flood it, but no longer tenanted. At one time it was claimed to be the lowest worked farm in Scotland, but now Lonnie, nearby, claims that doubtful privilege.

All is quiet now at Alturlie Point, but in the bad old days it was a favourite landing spot for smugglers. An ancient churchyard is still in evidence, but the stones are nearly all hidden in grass.

On the main road once again, my next stop was at Lower Cullernie, where we find an overgrown depression which is all that remains of an old tile works for making bricks and drain pipes at the beginning of this century. One of Cullernie's farm cottages, however, is roofed with tiles manufactured at this factory, and was inhabited then by a factory worker. The clay supplies decreased so much that it was finally considered uneconomical to carry on.

Standing is a large stone just discernible on the foreshore beyond the fields.

It is called Coinneach Odhar's Stone.

I had heard of the Abban Stone, and, having made extensive enquiries, soon discovered that they were one and the same. The story occurs in the Prophecies of the Brahan Seer, and he predicted that this immense stone, weighing at least eight tons and formerly marking the boundary of Culloden and Darnaway Estates, would be suddenly advanced as far into the sea as it lay inland, and no one would see it removed or be able to account for its sudden and marvellous transportation.

It actually did move on the 20th February 1799 a distance of 260 yards, and although some believed this to be the work of the Devil, the more probable explanation was that a large sheet of ice about eighteen inches thick had collected round the stone, which had helped to raise it in the tide and carried it the distance, aided by a terrific gale which blew from the land. The hole left after its removal was visible for many years afterwards.

According to George Bain's *Lordship of Petty*, the physical features of Petty reveal a series of striking transformations. First it formed part of the sea, and remains of fossilised sea mammals have been found far inland.

The sea subsided from these lands, leaving behind it depressions and numerous islands, today regarded as mounds and hillocks. In another transformation the plain became a marsh fed by fresh-water streams, gradually developing into a jungle with gigantic trees. Then peat mosses formed, and finally, moorland emerged, and man subsequently cultivated it to present-day standards.

About fifty to sixty years ago some ancient historic graves were dug up at Morayston, but the bones crumbled away when exposed to the air.

Taking a left turning at Petty War Memorial, beside the East Church, I came into the Dalziel district, split into the two farms of Easter and Wester Dalziel.

Of the three historic castles of Petty—Hallhill, Dalcross and Castle Stuart—only the two latter remain; and only the site of Hallhill is to be found at Wester Dalziel, on a mound now under regular cultivation. In comparatively recent times it was known as the Island, and marked as such on an old Winter's map dated 1760. But nobody in the district whom I met had ever heard of the Castle.

According to tradition, it was the residence of the De Moravia or Moray family before they went to Bothwell Castle; and it was destroyed by the Dunbars in 1508, when it belonged to the Ogilvies. After being rebuilt by them it was destroyed again on several instances. In all likelihood it met its final end at the hands of Cromwell's soldiers, who used Hallhill as barracks when stationed in the area.

25.   OLD FISHING DAYS

The road most familiar to the soldier in the neighbourhood of
Inverness is undoubtedly the one leading to Ardersier, as it is the route
taken by many a service man on his way back to barracks at Fort
George. To them it may have been a dreary country highway, but I am
going to prove the error of their misjudgment.

We branch off the main Inverness—Nairn road a little way before
reaching Newton hamlet, between there and the farm of Newton of
Petty; and the first we sight on our left is Lonnie, with the doubtful
honour of being the lowest worked farm in the Highlands.

At the road end leading to Lonnie a small stone bridge is hardly
noticeable, but is reputed by some to be haunted. An old story tells of
a practical joker who disguised himself as a ghost in a white sheet, and
lay in wait for a young ploughman who had gone to Newton smithy
with his plough irons. When the lad returned along the road, his
plough irons perched on his shoulder, the "ghost" rose up before him.

"Speak," he cried to the apparition, "or I will strike you with these
irons."

But the ghost remained silent, and in a rash moment the young man
brought the full weight of his plough irons down on the foolish fellow
inside the sheet, who fell dead on the bridge.

Part of the land down by the shore used to be known as The Canteen,
and a house, where Hugh Munro the shoemaker of bygone days lived,
also bore that name, but is no longer in existence. For a long time, I
believe, this stretch of ground was a sort of "no man's land" belonging
to neither of the adjacent proprietors.

Taking a dangerous bend on the road we find ourselves practically
in the farmyard of Scottach, or as it is more commonly known today,
Castle Stuart. Of course the reason of this change of name is due to its
proximity to one of Petty's two remaining castles, which was built
away back in 1623 or 1624 by Earl James Moray, son of the Bonnie
Earl, evictor of the Petty tenants. I am told that the Earls of Moray
never actually made it a family seat, though it is believed that they
stayed there periodically, probably on visits of business to Inverness.
It is recorded that when the Darnaway improvements were being
carried out, the joists of Castle Stuart were removed to be fitted into
the new building, but no use was made of them. For years the castle
stood roofless, but just over a century ago the eastern wing was made
habitable. Then for long it stayed unoccupied and unfurnished.
However, it has once again become inhabited.

Though ostensibly a private house, one room in the castle is set aside for the biennial collection of rents by the estate, presumably a clause in the lease. Apart from this room, occupied at other times of the year, there is another famous room which, according to tradition, hides the mystery of Castle Stuart. It is reputed to be haunted, but nobody has ever divulged the secret which lies within its walls.

A story tells of four local worthies who pledged themselves to sleep a night in the room, separately; but after their experience of a solitary vigil, none would speak of what occurred during the hours of darkness. As a result of his experience one of the braves went insane. Later, a drover, encamped nearby with some cattle, declared he was not afraid to break the seal of mystery, and volunteered to sleep a night in the haunted room. Next morning his body was found lying on the stone paving on the ground beneath the window where he had dared to spend the night.

The old walled garden used to extend to some thirty acres, but most of this ground is now included in the Scottach farmlands. As an example of compactness and security in time of danger we may yet find the stables and coachyard within the foundations of the castle.

Almost within a stone's-throw of the castle is the Established Kirk of Petty (West), on a site where a church has stood since St Columba founded it a thousand years ago.

The new Petty kirkyard lies outside the old walls, and when I passed up the grey cement steps, sprayed with confetti from a recent wedding, I was met with a sight so common in country churchyards today. It was a scene of overgrowth, and frankly I felt ashamed that neglect had taken a hold of so sacred a place as this.

Many very old flat tombstones adorn the path to the church door, and under the threshold of the church lie the remains of Big John MacGillivray of Dunmaglass, who led the MacKintosh clan at Culloden and died on the field, having killed fifteen Redcoats with his broadsword. It is said that his body, with many others, was buried in a trench and relatives and friends were forbidden to remove it. The Duke of Cumberland's troops kept watch over the graves for six weeks, but after that period they were left alone. When the trench was opened several ankers of whisky were poured into it, and the body of MacGillivray removed and reinterred at Petty Church.

At the east wing of the church I found the family vault of the MacKintoshes of Moy, a legacy from Lauchlan MacKintosh of Kinrara, seventeenth chief and author of the Kinrara MS, a history of the family. It was built at the end of the 17th century, and before then it seems the MacKintoshes were buried in a mausoleum inside the church itself. Actually Petty is the original home of the Mac-Kintoshes, chiefs of the Clan Chattan.

Another interesting vault has rather a unique origin, and although only built about fifty years ago, is almost hidden by a large ivy bush. In his will, a mason from Kerrowgair, one Charlie Campbell, left instructions that he should be buried in this vault, the door locked and the key thrown into Petty Bog.

The kirk originally had three galleries, but the one almost above the Table has been removed and another temporarily closed up. The floor-level pews can easily accommodate the congregation.

Outside again in the kirkyard I found the grave of Rev. John Morrison, better known as the Petty Seer, who became widely noted for his alleged prophecies and predictions, though more probably he was a man of shrewd natural gifts of observation and penetration. A book on his sayings and doings was published by A.B. MacLennan in 1894.

There are many stories told about him, but I like the one about his encounter with a number of fisherwomen returning from Inverness rather the worse for drink. Instead of rebuking them, he went into his manse and brought out his fiddle and made them dance a reel. They then went home the better for their exercise!

The tale of how he came to Petty is rather interesting. He is said to have given a warning to the Earl of Moray's factor, MacKenzie of Delvin, to come heavily armed on the next rent collection day, as the Frasers of Aird had conspired to murder him, as he had succeeded in recovering a debt payable to an Inverness merchant by a member of the Aird Frasers. In recognition of his services, the factor arranged the transfer of the minister to Petty.

Two mounds nearer the sea have been used as archery butts, but, according to local tradition, are claimed to be moot hills; and a little below Castle Stuart a sea-water mill, which may have been constructed by Cromwell's engineers, was in use until the early part of the 19th century. It was ingeniously designed to utilise the ebb and flow of the tide, and for many generations was considered to be one of the wonders of Petty.

The presence of local fishing fleets in the estuary of the Beauly Firth in the autumn, when they haunt home waters in pursuit of the popular Kessock herring, often brings to mind the fact that the communities now known as Westerton and Easterton, adjoining Balnaglack, were once made up of a district known as Fishertown, with a law and customs of its own. But, though the fisherfolk were many, the fishing was never very great in the vicinity, owing to the prevalence of fresh and salt water intermingling. The Petty fishermen did not like to stray far from home, so they kept up their crofts too.

In earlier days certain marked peculiarities developed in Fishertown. For instance, nobody was allowed to settle there without the permission of the whole community, and no one was allowed to marry out of the town. The holdings were held by crews, the headman being responsible for the payment of rent, often in kind, gathered from the land and not the sea.

There is something distinctively attractive about Ardersier, and holiday-makers return to it every summer. It must be one of the few Northern villages to retain thatched cottages lying in an area known as the Crook. However, the art of thatching is quickly dying out, and those householders who wish to retain this old-time appearance simply have to replace the thatch themselves.

Like many another fishing village in the Highlands, Ardersier has seen better days. Why, there was a time when the beach was literally black with fishing boats, and now scarcely a rowing boat is to be seen. A few of the older fisher folk still linger on, and you can recognise them in their polo-necked navy blue jerseys. I saw three old fishermen have a "news" on the jetty, now demolished, and judging by their glances in my direction I imagine that my ears might well have been burning. Aye, doubtlessly were some of the Ardersier worthies!

I gather the jetty had always been rather a "white elephant", as in the days of the fishing fleet the fishermen grudged the payment of harbour dues and consequently boycotted it. However, the credit of having had it built goes to the late Major Thomas Main, a son of the sea himself, who had the interests of his fellow-men at heart and was trying to render them a valuable service. I am told it was very handy in stormy weather when the sea was too rough to land the catches on the beach.

The coasters, using the Danish sea nets, have been responsible for cleaning up all these local fishing grounds, putting many smaller fishing communities out of business.

Although most of Ardersier is in a small parish of its own, the parish of Petty actually extends into the village as far as the Ship Inn.

The inn is over 200 years old and until 1912 was thatched with a very low roof. In that year it was slated; then a few years ago the whole place was rebuilt and modernised. From the three-storeyed store adjoining the inn farmers used to load their grain and potatoes directly on to the ships which were able to dock alongside. Latterly, fishing nets were kept in the store.

Until the First World War a popular ferry service was in operation between Chanonry Point and Fort George. I was told that the ferry was closed under rather unusual circumstances.

A local resident was attending a funeral, and, looking out into the bay he spied what appeared to be a periscope bobbing out of the water, then disappearing again. He drew the attention of a fellow mourner to it, who confirmed its identity. Later the matter was reported, enquiries made, and as no British submarines were known to be in the area at the time, the mysterious periscope was presumed to belong to the enemy. From then onwards passage to the Black Isle by water was considered unsafe, and the ferry was discontinued until the end of the war. However, it is no longer active.

Long before Fort George was built the village of Ardersier lay to the east of this peninsula and was known as Blacktown. The Government wanted to build a fort on the site of the Longman in Inverness, but the Town Council objected and refused to permit it. So it was decided that this piece of headland jutting into the Moray Firth would be an ideal position to build a fort. The land was purchased from the Cawdor estate, and the village of Blacktown was renamed Campbelltown, Campbell being the family name of the Earl of Cawdor. Fort George was founded in 1748, but not completed until 1767, when the garrison church was built.

A new village gradually grew up where we find Ardersier today, and practically nothing remains of the former village to the east of the fort. I believe the older folk still refer to their village as Campbelltown but the name was changed due to confusion arising between it and the town of that name in Kintyre.

The derivation of Ardersier is controversial. I was told that it meant "the place of the carpenters", though I am inclined to change that to the "point of the carpenters". It is also said to come from the Gaelic words "ard" and "ros" meaning "a high promontory". The parish was once known as the Parish of Six which rather suggests a low population! An old legend recalls the tale of a boatload of carpenters crossing the firth to Chanonry Cathedral being upset with the loss of all hands. There used to be quite a number of carpenters in the village, but the total today is nil.

On the right of the road to Fort George is Cromal Hill or Cromal Mount. The name Cromal is a contraction of Cromwell, and we find vestiges of Cromwellian days in the form of old forts within a few miles of Ardersier.

26.   CHEESE AND WHISKY

Leaving Ardersier by the back road, we fork at the war memorial and presently find ourselves in the steading of Ardersier Mains, now split up into smallholdings.

From there we can reach Hillhead, also broken up into holdings, and I think the most interesting of these, historically speaking, is now known as Kirkton. The byre was built from part of the original manse of Blacktown, and adjoining the steading is the old graveyard, only used now by families with lairs.

To the east of the church and manse we reach a flat stretch of land known as the Carse, where the farmland is sandy, and probably once covered with water.

At Baddock there was once a little briar bush which became widely known as Grant's Bush, and folk calling at the house for ceilidhs claimed they had seen a ghostly gathering round it.

Then there's the tale of the Baddock witch and her spell on the Thane of Cawdor of the 17th century, who was returning home from the Black Isle by way of Chanonry Ferry. As he passed by Baddock the witch is supposed to have cast her "evil eye" on him, and he had gone no farther than Drumdivan, near Kildrummie, when he dropped down dead. Consequently the witch, whether guilty or innocent, was burnt at the stake for her sins!

At the fork of the road to Lower Carse, near Baddock, an old inn stood, though no traces of it are to be seen today. However, occasionally a plough has struck its foundation. It is interesting to note in passing that within a small area around this inn nearly thirty illicit stills were once accounted for, scattered throughout the Carse woods.

The big sandy stretch on Whiteness Head guards the Lower Carse land from the sea, and among these level lying crofts is Leitchfield, named after an officer from Fort George who built this house. It was said he was such a good marksman that he could shoot and split an apple on his son's head. Another William Tell!

In spite of its sandy nature, Lower Carse can grow crops. In the last century, the year 1826 became known as "the year of the short corn", but when the corn was so short that it had to be pulled up by the roots in other areas, for some reason it grew well and long on Lower Carse, and the yield was naturally in great demand.

Among the crofts on the Muir of Balnagown are the remains of the first of two Cromwellian forts. It had lain hidden among trees for a number of years, but more recently came to light again when the wood was cut down. Again, it is gradually disappearing into oblivion since a young plantation has been built around it.

The other fort is to be found beside Milton of Balnagown, and both forts were probably used as shelters and are circular in shape.

Tomnathrach—"the hill of the serpents"—is a small hill on the Muir of Balnagown, and beside it I am told were old Danish earthworks. A story tells of two packmen fighting to their death on it, but perhaps more significant is the fact that it was used for "leaving changelings". According to a strange belief that fairies stole unbaptised babies and replaced them with old withered and discontented fairies in the form of a baby (called changelings), the parents concerned carried them to Tomnathrach in the hope of receiving back their own child.

At the end of the Lower Carse road a hundred yards or so from the point where it joins the main Ardersier—Nairn Road, we find the Kebbuck Stone, sheltering behind a local gamekeeper's house.

There are many conflicting tales about the Kebbuck Stone. Some say it had a connection with Prince Charlie—but was he ever in the district? Two clans were squabbling, and the Prince to settle the argument, sliced a kebbuck of cheese, and threw a half to the respective chiefs and bade each fight for the honour of his clan.

Again, it has been suggested that the stone is Druidical, and long ago when the sea flooded this area boats were moored to it. Fantasy?

Thirdly, the tale of a Campbell of Cawdor and a Rose of Kilravock attempting a runaway marriage against their parents' wishes, being caught at the stone, and an agreement made over biscuits and cheese!

Fanciful or farcical, these are the legends; but I'm inclined to believe the explanation given in Bain's *History of Nairnshire*, in which the author reveals the Kebbuck Stone as a relic of the Celtic church, and a typical church monument. Bain states that the outline of a Celtic cross can be made out on one side, though to me it seemed quite obliterated. A heap of stones, now dispersed, which lay beside the pillar were probably the ruins of an oratory.

From what, then, do we derive Kebbuck, the Scots word for cheese? There is no connection, according to Bain, as the word means "stone black". Scots folk have quite a fertile imagination!

The dog kennels attached to the 'keeper's house hide an unsolved mystery too: the two skeletons which still lie buried beneath the cement floor. When workmen discovered the first skeleton their find was immediately reported to the authorities, and their work held up considerably; so when the second came to light they quietly covered it up and got on with the job on hand! I wonder if there could be any connection between the skeletons and the two clan chiefs who fought at the Kebbuck Stone.

In a sixty-acre field of Wester Delnies close by, a number of wounded stragglers from Culloden died and are supposed to be buried in the west corner. In the days when horses ploughed the land, former farmers of Wester Delnies told their men to plough light in this part in case they disturbed the dead. However, in this mechanical age no bones have been unearthed! Long ago Wester Delnies was known as Fishertown of Delnies, and some of the older residents still remember boats on the beach.

Retracing our steps now back to Ardersier by a more direct route, we pass Milton of Balngown, which became famous as the home of a family of bonesetters, of whom Simon MacBean won world fame.

At Newton of Balnagown a crack in the gable-end of the house first divulged a secret chamber under the hearth of the kitchen. It had been used as a smuggling bothy, and it may be due to this hideout that the house has shrunk considerably into the ground, so that the window sills are practically level with the garden!

By the way, the fellow who made his own whisky downstairs was "caught in the act" and served a twelvemonth in jail. In those days it was quite customary for friends of the prisoners to visit the cells and bring food and drink. The story goes that the Newton Smuggler was visited one day by a group of his cronies, who brought with them plenty of their own home-brewed whisky, and before setting about their drunken orgy the following grace was said: "Oh, Lord, we thank Thee for such a place as this—but keep us out of it!"

27. GALLOW'S HILL

We have travelled as far as Tornagrain on the Nairn road, and so we take up from there towards the first cross-roads. To our left a side road branches to Dalcross aerodrome, the right one to Croy. There's little of importance on the former, but the Croy road has Midcoul, Hillhead and Lochindulty off it, which I feel bear mention in this chapter.

Until about 1880 Midcoul was run jointly with Culblair, the last tenant farmer being of the family of MacKessack; but since then they have been independent of one another, and William Rose has been farming at Midcoul for over forty years. He belongs to Dalcross and is among the few natives who can spin a yarn or two about Petty in the old days.

The hill known as Tom na Croiche behind his steading, he tells me, is reputed to be haunted, but though he has visited it at every time of day and night, "he has never seen anything worse than himself" Tom na Croiche means "gallows hill", and forms part of a ridge stretching east to the Culbin Sands.

Old Hillhead Quarry is now dormant, but from it the stones for all the buildings in Petty were taken, apart from modern houses, and once it was the only place in the plain of Petty where a solid rock surface was visible. The underlying rock is of red sandstone, but it is hidden by enormous fluvia-glacial deposits of sand, gravel and clay. In more recent times a new quarry has been opened near Cullaird, and is operated by the County Council.

Also at Hillhead is Lochindulty, practically dried up to a mere duck pond today, but I understand it was a recognised loch in former times. Beside it stood a croft, but the whole place appears as a wet marsh in the middle of one of the fields.

When Dalcross aerodrome was built at the beginning of the last war much good farming land was confiscated from the neighbouring farms, but the hundred acres taken from Culblair seem to have been little loss, as most of it was of a peaty and mossy nature.

The district we are now entering is commonly known as Breakley or Breachlich, and long ago, I understand, there was a host of crofts in and around Milton of Breachlich, and the folk living in them cut their peats on the flat lands of the present aerodrome. The railway line was built a little over a hundred years ago.

The Gollanfield cross-roads is among the most dangerous on the Nairn-Inverness thoroughfare, as it is often overlooked by the speedy motorist who likes to make the best of a five-mile stretch of straight highway. Consequently, on more than a single occasion, accidents have occurred. The railway line at Gollanfield has not been without blemish, and in 1953 two trains collided with the loss of three lives.

Between road and railway at Gollanfield we come to the farm of Balspardon where a fossilised tooth was found in one of the fields in 1921, forty feet above sea-level. Experts declared it belonged to a sea mammal, giving rise to the suggestion that water covered this district in early times. Another theory might be founded on the fact that whale carcasses washed ashore in the Moray Firth were carted by crofters and buried on their ground as a source of manure.

28. AROUND CULLODEN

I doubt if there's a bonnier sight than a field full of Highland
ponies with their foals at foot, and during the summer months this is
one of the fine pictures captured by the railway traveller as the south
train approaches Inverness. I am sure many a body has looked out of
the window and exclaimed:

"Ah, Highland ponies! We're really among the heather now!"

These ponies have actually been collected from many a Highland
croft, and come to Beechwood Farm for further marriage with the
Department of Agriculture's stallions kept there. The farm has been
Government owned since before the First World War and has been
the centre of Highland pony breeding for quite a long time.

This farm of Beechwood lies just off the main south road from
Inverness, and to reach it we branch off at Inshes. A quarter of a mile
past the farm, we approach Cradlehall, a place farmers at any rate
associate with another type of horse, the Clydesdale, and a man who
was renowned as the best known horse dealer in the north in his
generation, John Williamson.

In 1936 Mr Williamson introduced the Belgian breed into the
Highlands, but I do not think they ever got past the novelty stage with
the northern farmers. However, they proved enormously popular in
the south, being hardy, strong and steady animals.

The present farmhouse, I believe, is the Old Cradle Hall, which
gives the place its name. It must have been fairly small then, as two
wings have since been added. The old residence was built by General
Cauldfield, a commander at Fort George, who preferred the more
picturesque environments of the district to the salubrity of the ancient
fortress.

It is recorded that the General was lavishly hospitable, and the
victims of his hospitality were so often found laying incapable along
the roadway from the mansion house to Inverness that the General
decided he would have to stop the scandal of these drunken orgies. So
on the rafters above his dining-room he erected a row of bunks or
cradles, made a hole in the roof, and, by using a block and tackle,
hoisted the inebriated guests to greater heights until they became
sober!

Several modern bungalows have sprung up around Cradlehall in
recent years, and near the entrance to one of them is an old well,
overflowing into a roadside ditch, and it was here that a number of
English soldiers stopped to quench their thirst after Culloden and, it

is said, were killed while they drank.

We come next to Culloden Home Farm and Culloden House; the latter especially has close ties with the '45 Rebellion. The House stands on the site of Culloden Castle, and is historically important as having sheltered both Prince Charlie and the Duke of Cumberland within a few days. The Prince slept there (one of his few authentic resting places) the night before the battle. Then the Duke moved in, but made a longer visit!

In the dungeons, the only existing parts of the former castle, below the present house, seventeen officers of the Jacobite army were confined for three days, then taken outside and shot. Another story says they were hanged from an old tree in front of the house. No matter what may have been their end, they were undoubtedly murdered in cold blood by the order of that butcher Cumberland.

Near the entrance to Culloden House, an old tree stump used to carry a set of "branks" or Scold's Bridle, to which offenders were fixed, so that they could neither sit down nor stand erect. It was often used to "check the tongues of over-garrulous women", The tree fell about fifty years ago, the stump decayed, and has been replaced by a stone pillar. The "branks" have been removed elsewhere.

Culloden House was once the home of the Forbeses of Culloden, of whom Duncan Forbes, Lord President of the Court of Session was the most outstanding figure; and when the last of the heirs died over fifty years ago the claimants to the effects of Culloden House sold by public auction (lasting four days) every movable article in the house. They even took down the Adam and Eve statues on the main gates, but were obliged to return them to their rightful position as the heritable property of the estate.

Relics relative to Prince Charlie made fabulous sums. The dining-room table was sold to MacKintosh of MacKintosh for 375 guineas; the Prince's walking stick was purchased for Queen Victoria for £160; while his bed fetched £750. The total drawings amounted to over seven thousand pounds. Even the flower pots were sold from the greenhouses!

Tradition relates that for a number of years Culloden House had a secret—a mystery room. Locked and barred, it was for ever out of bounds for servants, guests and proprietor; and only before this sale were the bonds which hid the secret broken down.

The room lay dusty and empty, when at last the door was forced open, and placed in the centre of it was an old wooden (or stone) coffin, with the directions on it that it was to be buried at Chapelton burying-ground. However, by this time, no trace of the burying-ground remained, and was only remembered by some as a mound in the centre of one of the Chapelton fields. Each year, as it was ploughed, another furrow had encroached into the mound, until eventually the whole hillock was taken into cultivation. So the coffin was borne to the family graveyard, three-quarters of a mile from Culloden House, and laid to rest in the vault.

The village of Balloch lies a little way to the east of Culloden House, and if you knew it before the First War, you would scarcely recognise it today. Gone are the thatched cottages, the school with the latticed windows and the Kerrow Road (once a county bypass). It's now known as the Green Road, so overgrown it has become.

Perhaps the man who saw the most changes in his line of business was John Bruce, the blacksmith. He came to Balloch in 1912, and between the two wars, he told me, he had something like 400 horses to keep shod.

When he came here there was a cartwright, a shoemaker and a tailor, and you could buy a suit of clothes, made from the best of cloth, for fifty shillings. David Anderson, son of the last Balloch tailor, still keeps up the family home and his horticultural efforts are certainly a great asset to the beauty of the village.

Ascending the brae from Balloch and travelling in the direction of Culloden we come to a collection of small-holdings.

Much of this district has been taken over by the Forestry Commission. At one time, I am told, the sea covered much of this land, even on the brae-face, as traces of water marks and shells have been found at a considerable height. It is certain at any rate, that the area around Feabuie was very swampy, and the original pioneers of not so long ago had to do much drainage and hand tillage before crops would grow. In fact, water from this swamp was taken in burns to lime kilns on the firth shore.

The name Feabuie is a shortened version of the Gaelic *fhear bhuie*, meaning "the yellow man", and the story I've always heard is about a foreigner—maybe a Chinaman—who first came to stay in the district, having landed off a boat.

Highwood Forest between here and the firth was once good agricultural land, and when it was cut down during the last war remnants of old dykes were found by the foresters, and wells can still be seen in some places. The old people knew the names of the places—all Gaelic names—but I imagine they are mostly forgotten now. Highwood has been replanted lately.

Another derivation of the name Feabuie is given as "the yellow marsh".

At the farthest east point of Feabuie there is rather an interesting well at a point where the three estates of Culloden, Dalcross and Darnaway meet; and it is said that this is the only spot where the proprietors of the respective estates can drink together while still standing on their own property!

29. CULLODEN MEMORIES

The most popular excursion within easy distance of Inverness, among the tourists who come to the Highlands, is undoubtedly to Culloden Moor and the scene of the famous battle.

It is at the Tower of Culloden we make out first halt; little to be known about it. It is post-Culloden, built by a member of the family of MacKintoshes of Raigmore in memory of the battle.

Old cabbies bringing tourists to the battlefield in the days of horse transport loved to stop outside and spin the yarns of their imagination, about it being a State Prison during the '45 or a guiding sentinel for ships sailing up the Moray Firth. All pure fiction!

However, since those days, the Tower has changed its appearance, the result of extensive renovations which have turned the "fort" into an ideal home with a modern setting.

You have to go down past Blackpark Farm to reach the Clooty Well, which attracts hosts of "well-wishers" on the first Sunday of May every year.

It was originally known as St Mary's Well, and when analysed some years ago, the water was found to be the second purest in Scotland. One of the Forbeses of Culloden decided that it was an ideal place to have a bath, and persuaded her husband to build a wall round it to give privacy.

It later became known locally as a fairy well, and at Beltane (first day of May) it became customary for people to visit the well, leave food, drink and a piece of rag tied on the Clooty tree beside the well (clothing for the fairies). They then wished a wish, and went home. Now the modern idea is to leave money, and it has been more recently commercialised, the money being collected in the well and distributed among charitable organisations. As they wish a wish the visitors tie their pieces of rags (or cloots) on any available tree, so that some twenty neighbouring trees are thus adorned, and everybody is happy except those who have to clear up the litter afterwards!

About a hundred years ago the capercailzie (wood grouse) had become almost extinct in the Highlands, but was reintroduced into various areas. Today in the woods above Blackpark this breed of bird has become fairly common, and seems to be more plentiful here than in any other part of the vicinity.

The next place worthy of a visit is the cottage known as King's Stables to the west of the battlefield.

It was inhabited until about fifty years ago. It was always a snug little place with wooden rafters, a clay floor and an open fireplace. Some of the English soldiers stabled their horses here after the battle.

Stable Hollow is some little way from King's Stables, and as the name suggests, is in a hollow to the east of them. The old road went through it. A large boulder at the back of Stable Hollow House may have had some connection with Prince Charlie—some say he stood on it!—and a smaller stone with an almost obliterated date and design bears the name "G. Bruce" and lies a few yards from the front door. This latter stone may be comparatively modern, but no known identification of the holder of that name has ever been discovered.

I have early memories of a visit to Culloden Cairn on the 16th April on several occasions during my school Easter holidays, to attend the memorial service with my kilted father on the anniversary of Culloden. I have never managed to take part in this act of remembrance since, though often have I passed through the recognised battlefield.

A retired doctor I met during my travels tried to convince me that nothing more than a small fray took place at Culloden, and that the facts of the battle are mere fictional traditions of an imaginative race! Fortunately, we do not all think alike, and if we believe in history at all there is no reason to doubt the great tragedy of Culloden.

The Cairn is built of rough stones, and responsible for its erection was Duncan Forbes of Culloden, grand-uncle of the present proprietor. Built into the Cairn is rather a remarkable inscribed stone, which requires a little explanation when we read:
"Culloden, 1746—E.P. fecit 1858."
It was carved by a commercial traveller, Edward Power, an enthusiastic Jacobite, and was intended for another cairn begun in 1858 but never finished.

The story of the Battle of Culloden has been described by authors innumerable in novels, historical articles and guide books, but I feel I cannot just pass by without making mention of it.

While the Highland army was lying at Inverness, the Duke of Cumberland and his English army were marching northwards by Aberdeen, and on the 14th April 1746 reached the town of Nairn. On that day Prince Charlie left the Highland Capital and took up residence at Culloden House.

The following morning the Prince drew up his army on Culloden Moor and awaited the approach of the enemy, but meanwhile the Duke of Cumberland had ordered a day of festivity to celebrate his birthday, and the Highlanders waited in vain. However, realising the cause of the delay, the Prince decided to attack by surprise the Redcoated invaders encamped at Nairn, and mustered his clansmen together, appointing the hour of 2 a.m. as zero hour for the attack. The Highlanders set out that evening in two columns at some distance from one another and, in trying to keep clear of the public highway, presently found themselves toiling through boggy land which held them up so much that when the intended hour of attack arrived they had only reached Kilravock, four miles from the English camp. A halt was called, and finally it was decided to retreat before the day should break.

Tired and dejected the Highlanders returned to Culloden, and, by this time, supplies of food and drink had shrunk to a bare minimum so that even the Prince himself could find nothing better than a morsel of bread and a glass of whisky to satisfy his appetite. Some foraging parties returned with food, but before it could be cooked Cumberland's army was seen approaching in the distance across the plain.

The Highlanders were drawn up in two lines, the right commanded by Lord George Murray consisting of Athole men, Camerons, Stewarts, Frasers, MacKintoshes, Farquharsons and others. On the left, commanded by Lord John Drummond were the MacDonalds of Clanranald, Keppoch and Glengarry. The latter caused much dissension in the Highland army, as the MacDonalds always claimed the privilege of being on the right line, and this oversight in position gave them grave offence.

The Hanoverians were obviously the stronger army with a body of cavalry on each wing and artillery between every two regiments in the front line, so the poor Highlanders had little chance of success from the beginning. However, they fired the first shots, which proved ineffective and were returned more sharply, killing many a kilted warrior. A well-aimed shot narrowly missed the Prince, covering him with dust, and killing his servant, leading a spare horse. For nearly an hour the artillery kept firing, the Highlanders standing up to the barrage badly, and at last a message was sent to the Prince begging permission to attack. But before the order could be given the MacKintoshes broke from the ranks and charged madly towards the enemy, followed by the whole right line. At first the charge seemed successful until the Highlanders realised that the broken English line was backed by another. Their efforts soon weakened, and their fury was quickly spent. Only the left wing could possibly have saved the day, but the offended MacDonalds preferred to suffer defeat rather than forgive the insult, and stood in their column slashing the heather with their broadswords. As the enemy approached they turned their backs and marched off the field in good order! Then followed the final retreat of straggling Highlanders pursued in every direction by bloodthirsty Redcoats.

The Prince, who had watched the battle from a stance beside a lonely elm tree at Balvraid (still standing though now partly hollow), was soon speeding westwards on horseback with a few of his trusted followers through Strathnairn and Stratherrick and ultimately into the hills to take refuge till he finally gave up hope of winning a Crown and embarked for France.

The Duke of Cumberland is reputed to have watched the battle from a large boulder to the east of the battlefield, now known as Cumberland's Stone. He may have stood beside it on horseback, but one belief is that he stood on it and left an imprint on its grey surface!

The graves of the clans have been clearly marked after research into local traditions by Forbes of Culloden, and their identity is believed to be as accurate as can possibly be.

Near the Well of the Dead Big John MacGillivray fell dying, and a stone commemorates the spot.

Leanach is a typical cottage in existence during the battle, and, according to tradition, a cannon ball fell into the house through the chimney, and smashed the bottom out of an old metal pot hung over the fire. An elderly lady, Miss Bell MacDonald, occupied this cottage until her death in 1912, aged 83, and I am told her grandmother was a little girl living in another house during the battle.

Many are the traditions and stories of the battle's aftermath, and one rather delightful tale tells how the Prince sought refuge in Culloden House before making his hasty retreat westwards. The Redcoats were soon on his track, but failed to recognise the sonsy wench in the kitchen as the Prince. As they entered, the head cook flung a haddock at the Prince with the words: "Get on with your work, you lazy woman," and so skilfully did she do it that the soldiers were completely taken in and the Prince was able to escape unnoticed.

30.   THE HARD LANDS

The district beyond Culloden Battlefield consists mostly of crofts, but a small community has arisen around Culloden Moor Station.

On the farm of Cantraybruiach can be found a collection of Druid stones near the banks of the River Nairn, but they are not on a par with the Clava Circles.

There have been Dallases at Wester Brae of Cantray for over 500 years, and one of the family was a magistrate in Inverness at the last trial of witches in Scotland. Young Hugh Dallas inherited the farm from his uncle who died in 1940.

But it is before we come to this Dallas inheritance that we take a fork to the left to reach Dalcross Castle, which was built about 1622-24, at the same time as Castle Stuart.

It appears to have been built by the eighth Lord Lovat for his second wife, a daughter of Lord James Stuart of Doune, so that she could be near her cousin, the Earl of Moray, at Castle Stuart. But she never lived in it as she died before its completion.

According to the author of the Wardlaw MS., Rev. James Fraser, all the freestone for the building of Dalcross Castle was taken from Covesea, near Elgin, and the wood for the beams from Dalcathaig, which might well mean that there is not a better timbered house in Moray or Nairn. For a time it was owned by a Major Bateman, a Cromwellian officer, a noted figure in his day; then by a Bailie Dunbar of Inverness, a money-lender; until it came into the hands of Mackintosh of Mackintosh in 1702. After that it fell into ruins.

It was rebuilt by the late Major MacAndrew about 1900. He had it on lease, and after he died, Captain Henry Alford took over and added an annexe. He did not stay very long, and was followed by various owners, including Fraser Simpson, the composer, who died in it.

The most remarkable event in the castle's history, some say, was the funeral of one of the Mackintosh chiefs in 1731. Having died at Moy, this laird's body was brought to Dalcross Castle, where it lay in state for exactly two months and two days, and during this period an "open house" was kept for all and sundry. The funeral expenses amounted to an enormous sum.

The reason for the delay was the awaited arrival of the next heir, a Mackintosh of Daviot, who was abroad at the time—and it was against all Highland etiquette to proceed with the funeral without his presence! Some 4,000 mourners attended the funeral (3,000 of them armed) and they extended in a long line from Dalcross to Petty Churchyard in the funeral procession—a distance of four miles!

The farm of Little Dalcross has an interesting association with Culloden, and it is thanks to the Duke of Cumberland's army treading heavily over a new-sown cornfield, that Highland farmers now roll their crops! According to history, the corn was so badly trampled that the farmer despaired of his crop, but when it brairded and ripened the yield was the best ever harvested at any time before or since! The field is quite close to the steading, and a group of trees within its acreage are a treasured landmark that is not allowed to be removed, although one tree fell in recent gales. It is believed that the English cannon fired at Dalcross Castle from the shelter of these trees, and a well aimed cannon ball has left its mark above the front door.

A mound in one of the Hardhill fields has Druidical associations.

I heard here the tale of the Whispering Stone; I understand this stone, usually known by a Gaelic name, can be found a little way west of the village. However, I have since learned that the stone in question is not at Croy, but at Rigoul, nearer Rait Castle.

There is much controversy about the derivation of the name Croy. A former statistical account writer suggests that it comes from the French *croix*, meaning "cross", and that the neighbouring Dalcross is derived from the French *de la croix*—"of the cross". However, an enthusiastic Gaelic scholar, prefers to think that the name is derived from his own mother tongue. The nature of the fine farming land in the district is fairly firm, and this may have given rise to the Gaelic word *cruaidh*, meaning hard, from which we get the name Croy.

Croy Church was built in 1767, and accordingly, I take it, a former church stood on the same site. A stone in one of the gables bears the inscription 17TM67. Extensive repairs have been carried out since. The present building has been in continuous use for nearly 200 years, and its bell is older still, as a minute in the Session Record of 1688 states: "The Kirk Bell was com hom from London in a new cast."

31. ROYAL VISITORS

The village of Croy includes two county boundaries, and is thus divided between Inverness-shire and Nairnshire; so by taking the Clephanton road we find ourselves well into the latter county, and the estate of Kilravock.

The Roses of Kilravock have played an important part in the history of Nairnshire, being one of the oldest families, and Kilravock Castle is the ancestral home of the chiefs of that clan. In fact, it has been occupied by successive generations of Roses since its foundation in 1460, and is the second castle to have stood on that site. The first is believed to have been founded in 1275.

Only twice in the family lineage has the male line been broken, coincidentally by representatives of the same name, Elizabeth Rose. The first Mrs Elizabeth Rose was one of the most remarkable women of her time in the North of Scotland, and no stranger of note visited the district without being entertained by her. It was during her residence that Robert Burns called at Kilravock in the autumn of 1787, breakfasted with Mrs Rose and her mother, and later in the day visited Kildrummie.

The present chief, Miss Elizabeth Rose, succeeded to the title on the death on active service of her brother in the last war, and by his premature death the male line of chieftains was once again broken. I believe that the famous gooseberry bush in the old Tower of Kilravock has withered away too, perhaps fulfilling a family tradition that the bush would only flourish with the male line of heirs.

In the year 1562, Mary Queen of Scots, as a young widow of twenty years, visited Inverness. Although her mother had been in the North seven years earlier, it was the first time the young Queen had come to her Highland dominions. She stayed four days in Inverness, and on her homeward journey spent the first night at Kilravock Castle, where one of the rooms is still known as Queen Mary's Room.

While staying in Inverness prior to the Battle of Culloden, Prince Charles dined at Kilravock and was entertained by Baron Kilravock, himself a staunch Hanoverian, who played to him on the fiddle. The fiddle and a punch bowl used by the Prince are treasured family relics in the castle yet.

The next day when the Duke of Cumberland passed by the castle, Kilravock was at the gates to receive him.

"So I understand you had my cousin, Charles, here yesterday," the Duke hailed him.

"Yes, please your Highness," replied Kilravock; "not having an armed force I could not prevent him."

"You did perfectly right," said the Duke, "and I entirely approve of your conduct."

So saying he rode on to Culloden Moor to meet his cousin.

If you belong to that district east of Croy you probably will have heard of Jock Stott the smuggler. I came across his house at Easter Balcroy, or rather the cottage which has been renovated from his hovel. When it was reconditioned after Jock died more than eighty years ago, tradesmen found quite a treasure of "still" material used by this master-smuggler under the lobby.

There's a story told that when Jock was in the act of making his own brew, he would climb a nearby tree, and wave a large white sheet shouting: "There's only one way!"

Naturally, the local folk kept well out of his sight, thinking he must be daft—and that was just what he wanted!

Another tale tells about the arrival of the excisemen, who met Jock's wife on their way to his house, and demanded that she should lead them to his still. She agreed, then took them through heather, marsh and thorns, till eventually they came out into the open in front of Brackla Distillery, to which she pointed triumphantly: "That's the still over there!"

Kilravock Mill is quite a landmark in the district, and the north gable end bears the initials HR MF and the date 1641 Having consulted George Bain's *History of Nairnshire*, I note that in 1611 Hugh, Baron of Kilravock, succeeded to the title, and married Magdalene Fraser of Strichen, and I think they provide the answer to the mill gable riddle. The other gable was built at a later date, 1733, and bears the initials HR JR—another Hugh Rose and his second wife. Jean Rose—separated with the floral emblem of a rose.

The River Nairn, which passes close by the farm of Milton, supplied the water for the mill, and was dammed about three hundred yards upstream to allow the water to flow towards the mill and actually pass underneath the farm steading. Time has worn away the dam, and the path of this stream is now completely dried up.

Recalling for a moment the tragic defeat of Culloden, tradition records that on returning from his visit to Kilravock, it was suggested to Prince Charles that an attack should be made on the Royalist camp at Balblair, near Nairn. Many of the officers advised against such a plan, but the Prince gave peremptory orders and the Highland army set off for Nairn, marching in two columns.

The first, composed of the Clans, was led by Lord George Murray, and the second, consisting mainly of Lowland regiments, by the Earl of Perth. The first column had orders to cross the river about three miles from Nairn, and then lower down to recross, and attack the Hanoverians in flank and rear, coming out by Broadley or Firhall. The second column was to make its attack from the west, keeping close to the coast road and by following these instructions it would come out at Tradespark. By zero hour the advanced column had only reached Knockanbuie on the Kilravock'estate, and the leaders called a halt.

It has been said by a wag that if Prince Charlie had slept in all the houses and caves where he is reputed to have rested, he would be living yet! So not unnaturally the origin of the Loch of the Clans and the surrounding Moor of the Clans has been credited to him. However, it seems strange that in the 1796 Statistical Account, the Rev. Hugh Calder, minister of Croy, should write these words only fifty years after the battle of Culloden:

"There is óne lake called Loch of the Clans, but for what reason it goes by this name is not known. It is about a mile long . . . "

A lake dwelling was discovered at the Loch of the Clans in 1863. A few arrow heads and flints were found in the vicinity, and a cairn on its site is believed to have formed an islet in the loch. The cairn stood on a mound, and investigations disclosed that this mound was artificial and stood on wooden piles and stones.

The island may have been a leper-house, and that the Loch of the Clans has been derived from the Gaelic *loch na cloimhean*—"the loch of the lepers".

32.   INTO NAIRN

The farmhouse of Meikle Kildrummie is not a new building and still retains some old period characteristics, such as the crow-step gable ends, which are quite unique in the district. It was to this house that Robert Burns came on a visit in 1787, accompanied by Mrs Elizabeth Grant of Kilravock and Mrs Grant, the minister's wife, and listened to a recital of Gaelic songs.

The library in the house at the time contained a wonderful selection of the classics, and, no doubt, had Burns glanced through the volumes he might have been amazed at finding such high-class literature in a farmhouse.

Howford Bridge was built across the River Nairn in 1905, and encased in the stone pillars, I am told, are coins of the day, a Nairnshire newspaper and a bottle of whisky. The stones were carted to the scene of building operations by local crofters.

Balblair House has grown in dimensions since the Duke of Cumberland's officers stayed there before Culloden, and no date is known of its original construction. It was definitely existing in the 17th century, and in 1746 was probably thatched and fairly small.

By looking around at Balblair it is easy to understand the advantage of Cumberland's choice of encampment. On the south the ridge of Kildrummie afforded excellent shelter for his troops; and the swamp in the foreground was ample protection.

At the gateway to Nairn we find old Newton House, now a hotel, but at the turn of the century it was bought by Sir Robert Finlay, M.P. for Nairn, who was not only a lawyer of repute but internationally famous as a jurist. He became Lord Chancellor and was raised to the peerage as Viscount Finlay. His son also became a judge in the English courts. During his lifetime Viscount Finlay took a keen interest in the local golf club, and leased the links on his property to them at the nominal fee of one shilling per annum. In his will he left the land to the club, and likewise the agricultural showground was left to the Nairnshire Farming Society.

The old name for Nairn was Invernairn, because it stood at the mouth of the River Nairn, and if we study an old map of the town we shall see that the original town consisted of one street called Main Street (now High Street), running parallel with the river. The houses ran at right angles to the street, so the residents could easily reach the river, their only source of water.

You will find an 1821 map of the town in the Jury Room of the

County Buildings, and this copy was discovered by a London book dealer in an old library, and offered to the management of the *Nairnshire Telegraph*, who purchased it and presented it to the town.

At one time the burgh was divided into two parts, with English the language spoken in the Fishertown, and Gaelic the common tongue elsehwere. The Fishertown folk were distinctly Norse, and some families, I believe, still bear the Norse features.

This district at the north end of the town came into being as the result of making a harbour suitable for fishing boats. Before that time there were two fishing villages a little to the east and west of the river mouth. The west Fishertown was known as Fishertown of Delnies and the prevailing family here was MacKintosh; while to the east at Cothill the chief family was Main, this particularly being of Norse origin.

In past days the Michaelmas markets were very popular, and farm produce was sold at Shambles Yard, now the site of the Congregational Church. The cattle were exposed on the Links, and there was a Horse Wynd somewhere in the region of Bridge Street.

The chief attraction in Nairn is the beach, with its long expanses of sand to the east of the harbour, and in summer you will find an excellent caravan and camping site with sanitation facilities. The west beach is subject to erosion and is not as sandy as in past days.

Then, of course, there is golf with two fine links, and many championships have been won on the Nairn links.

So far I have not mentioned the historical background of Nairn, but I must confess that I was disappointed to find that the Royal Burgh is strangely void of any really old buildings. Gone are the Castle of Nairn and the old Kirk of the Holy Rood, which stood not far away. The Cawdor Estate office is built on the site of the castle, and the original castle, it is said, was probably built of timber.

King William the Lion is believed to have stayed in the castle when he came north in 1179 to quell an insurrection in Ross, and some think he may have built it. It was here that he took the submission of the Earl of Orkney, and it was for long in the hands of a constable, who held it for the King.

In 1562 Queen Mary passed through Nairn on her way to Inverness; and in 1645 Montrose's men, after the Battle of Auldearn, pursued some of the fleeing Covenanters to Nairn and burned down some of the houses in the town.

While in Nairn the Duke of Cumberland stayed in Kilravock Town House (now non-existent) prior to the Battle of Culloden, and in 1773 Dr Johnson and Boswell visited the town, and saw for the first time a peat fire, and heard the spoken Gaelic tongue. Some folk allege that Robert Burns visited Nairn, but in his *History of Nairnshire*, George Bain emphatically states:

"The poet Burns did not visit the town of Nairn. In coming from Strathspey he had crossed to Kilravock by way of the Bridge of Dulsie and General Wade's Road. His visit to Kilravock over, he proceeded to Inverness and went to see the Falls of Foyers."

The writer is usually reliable.

33. STONES OF ANCIENT DAYS

It is a fair jump from Nairn to Daviot, but at this point I feel it is a step we must take, and return again to Nairn by way of Cawdor. Actually, in this chapter we don't really touch Daviot village, but branch off the main road eastwards opposite Balvonie Farm, and presently find ourselves in part of that district known as Nairnside.

Very little remains of Castle Daviot, as the stones through time have been borrowed to erect other buildings. Most of the farm steading of Daviot Mains originated here, I believe, as also did the garden wall. Until it was destroyed in 1534 by Hector MacKintosh of MacKintosh, the old castle was a stately and massive structure, standing about two hundred yards from the site of the more modern Daviot House, built by Alexander MacKintosh, twenty-fourth chief, about 1820. A strong wall enclosed about 300 square yards with four round vaulted towers, one at each corner. These towers were three storeys high and secret passages led through the main walls to the vaulted guardroom overlooking the drawbridge across the moat.

Down by the River Nairn, in one of the Daviot Mains fields are a number of stone circles, vestiges of the Druids, and being in line with the Clava Circles, may be in some way linked up with them.

Back to Nairnside we travel towards Leanach, passing the sandstone quarry from where the stones were taken for the building of the Culloden viaduct. Clava Lodge close by is a comparatively modern building compared with the neighbouring dwellings known as the Clava Circles, consisting of a group of three, in a wonderful state of preservation. Being some two thousand years old, they belong to the Neolithic age, but it is a matter of controversy whether or not they are burial places.

As I strode through this ancient "village" of Druidical days, surrounded by the foliage of rowan, elm, oak and birch, one August afternoon, the whirr of a farmer's binder brought my thoughts back to modern times. What a comparison, I thought: if only these stones could talk!

A cup-mark stone, rescued from the roadside, forms part of Balnuarin farmhouse garden wall, but there are many such stones in the district. The total in Scotland is 204. Of this number Nairnshire can claim 60, and Inverness-shire 43. At Clava alone there are 22 cupped stones.

Nothing very much is known about these cup-mark stones and suggestions of their origin may be that they were records of occurrences such as births; sacrificial cups; or had something to do with sun-worship.

An old Druid burying ground was excavated recently on Culdoich Farm, but little of consequence was found—except bones!

According to tradition a giant boulder was carried down the Great Glen by glacial action in the ice-age, but split up. Laggan claims to possess one slice, Croygorston, near Clava, the other. The local legend of the Croygorston specimen tells of a witch who carried a large stone down towards Croygorston in her apron, but her apron-strings broke, and the stone rolled down the hillside gathering in immensity as well as speed till it finally rested where it can still be seen today.

Yes, and every time it hears the cock crow—it turns round. A perfectly true statement—because the stone naturally cannot hear!

Dalroy Burn contains some wonderful pebbles, and before the First War, a manganese deposit was mined for use in making explosives. Although eighteen feet deep, it was not an economical proposition when deposits were discovered elsewhere.

We are retracing our steps towards Daviot again, this time on the south side of the River Nairn, and if I were to speak about the *Cailleach an t-siuga* to folk who knew this district in past days, they would immediately think of the MacGillivray's wee shoppie at the Castletown cross-roads. It was a popular meeting place for the community, and, although not a licensed bar, you could be sure of getting a wee dram (home-brewed) to help you on your way! It was the only house in the district with a clock, and people came from miles to learn the time.

Castletown had its castle, though little is known about it. The Calders at Castletown Farm told me the name given to it was "Mattoch". Only the site remains, but excavations on a small scale resulted in little information except that the castle was built of sandstone. The nearest sandstone quarry is at Leanach, on the other side of the River Nairn. A moat around the castle site is still evident and fills with water in wet weather.

An ancient burying ground in the Castletown fields, partly hidden by stones collected off the fields during cultivations, is locally known as the Crothan and may have had something to do with Castle Mattoch. Two large stone pillars, farther west, which were removed to widen the roadway some years ago, were believed to mark the entrance drive leading to the castle.

34. ECHOES OF CAWDOR

As a farm I do not think Kirkton of Barevan is very unusual; but behind the steading and farmhouse we find the ruins of the old Cawdor Church and Barevan Churchyard. The church was the Parish Church of Cawdor until 1619, when Sir John Campbell of Cawdor, in fulfilment of a vow made by him when in danger of shipwreck in returning from Islay, built the existing Parish Church of Cawdor. Until then Barevan was the burying ground of the Cawdor family and the Campbells of Clunas.

Only the walls of the church remain at Barevan, and the turf-covered floor is flagged with tombstones, several of them bearing fine examples of cup-marks. The last burial to take place in the kirkyard was in 1933, and the grave is included within the church enclosure.

Beyond the east gable end of the church is a rather curious stone coffin, where according to tradition, suspected witches were laid and covered with a heavy stone lid. If the lid could be removed by them their innocence was proved, but I am inclined to think that many an innocent victim succumbed to suffocation owing to lack of strength.

Beside the coffin, now devoid of lid, I found a large round stone, which I imagine is the stone carried there in a tartan plaid from the Cawdor burn a mile distant by a man of 74. The story tells that he threw it over the kirkyard gate with the words: "That'll give them something to lift!"

The original Cawdor manse was situated at Riereach, and I believe part of the barn was built from one of the manse walls. However, the new kirk of Cawdor was built before the manse, and the minister had a considerable distance to travel for his services. Consequently we find he took short-cuts, and one ford on the Cawdor burn is still appropriately known as the Minister's Leap!

At the time of Culloden a young herd boy from Riereach, attracted by the sound of gunfire, climbed to the top of Tor-buiach, a small promontory not far from Easter Galcantray, and watched the battle in progress. He then ran back for a meal, and later in the evening was so curious that he went down to the battlefield to get a closer look. Spotted by some English soldiers, he was captured and questioned and detained until the following Monday engaged in digging graves. His payment was a MacGillivray tartan kilt, which he took back to his employer; and it is believed that the kilt or part of it is still in existence.

We have wandered a little farther than I intended, because I felt it more practical to mention Riereach at this stage. So let us retrace our steps to a fork in the road to the right, and reach Auchindoune, at the foot of the Hill of Doune, a typical example of the old vitrified forts. The discovery of cist graves was made in 1878 at Auchindoune on the lower slopes of the Hill of Doune, and some of these graves, brought up in the course of ploughing, were within a few inches of the surface of the ground. A pottery urn was also discovered in a deeper grave, and was ornamented by markings made in the clay by a sharp instrument.

The top of the Doune is cup-shaped, and the soil is a rich dark loam, which may have been due to the debris of food thrown out by those who had occupied the fort in prehistoric days.

Cawdor village has been described by some writers as the prettiest village in Scotland. It certainly has an old-fashioned glamour of its own. It's a homely community, indeed, but perhaps we can expect little else, because it's a place with a common interest — the Cawdor estate.

Until the 14th century the Thanes of Cawdor lived in the Castle of Nairn, with a small country seat at Old Calder, about half a mile north of the present Cawdor Castle. Early in the next century, William Thane of Cawdor was page to James II, and later became a king's favourite, rising to the position of Chamberlain for the King north of the Spey, besides other honours. I am told that his carefully kept books are still preserved in the castle.

According to an old document dated 1454, we learn that Thane William was granted a licence to build a castle at Cawdor with walls, moats and iron portcullis, and to fortify it with turrets and other defensive ornaments and apparatus. The licence granted, where would he build? His answer was not only original but unique.

Placing a gold chest, containing the workmen's wages, on the back of a donkey, he sent off the little grey animal to choose its own site, and according to tradition he decided to build the castle where the donkey rested. Under its heavy weight the donkey did not travel very far, and when it came to three thorn trees, it selected the middle one and lay down beside it; and there, around the thorn tree, Thane William built his castle.

Down in the basement or dungeon you will still see the little thorn tree protected by an iron railing and the gold chest beside it! Ten years after building the castle Thane William died.

Until this time the name of the Cawdor family was Calder, and it is not until the end of the 15th century that we hear about the Campbells, the family name of the present Earl of Cawdor. By then the Thanes of Cawdor had become the most influential and richest family in Scotland, but constantly at feud with their neighbours, particularly the Roses of Kilravock. In 1492 a grandson of Thane William (who built the Castle) married Isabel, daughter of Kilravock, but their first child died in infancy. The father died before the birth of the second daughter Muriel, and this young lady appears to have been the cause of a great upheaval in the family through no fault of her own.

At this stage Campbell of Argyll got himself appointed co-guardian of Muriel (then in infancy and heiress to the Cawdor estate) with Lady Kilravock. In 1499 he sent Campbell of Inverliver, with sixty men, to carry off the child. The grandmother, realising the motive of the abduction, and fearing trickery on the part of the Campbells, thrust the key of her coffer into the fire and branded the child on her thigh for future identification of the proper heiress. An alternative tradition states that the child's nurse bit the tip off a finger.

The baby was seized and despatched, in the care of six men, ahead of the main body of invaders, while the others dawdled in the rear with a dummy — a sheaf of corn disguised as the child. Soon Alexander and Hugh Calder, uncles of the babe, with a strong force caught up with the Campbells and a fierce battle ensured in the neighbourhood of Daltulich; but the child escaped unharmed with her abductors. In 1510, Muriel Calder married Sir John Campbell at the tender age of thirteen, and lived happily ever after. So the Campbells came to Cawdor.

The first Baron Cawdor rose to that honour in 1796.

Few churches are as interesting as Cawdor Parish Church. The porch, belfry and the part of the parish church facing east and west are probably original. The other wing is more recent. On the porch the chained jougs remind us of past punishments when offenders were tied by the neck and ridiculed for their sins. The old-fashioned collection ladles may be reminiscent of the stick and feather days, when the beadle went round the sleeping members of the congregation to waken them up! These ladles are the few still in use today.

The Communion Cups or Chalices are dated 1619, and were presented to the church by the Laird of Cawdor of that day. They are exceptionally fine and hand-beaten. Two of the cups have been on show at an exhibition of church plate in Edinburgh.

The old church records from 1619-1719 were burned in a fire, but a copy of them from that date onwards is well preserved in the manse. Can many churches produce such ancient records of their sessions?

A more recent addition to the valuable possessions of Cawdor Church is the Communion Table, made by estate workers from the wood of a 250-year-old walnut tree blown down in the Castle grounds.

35.   LONELY GRAVES

On the Rosefield road on the east boundary of Cawdor village I found an interesting old meal mill dated 1635. The mill looked its age and was formerly a combined meal and barley mill; and flour was produced more than meal about ninety years ago until the local folk decided it was cheaper to buy from the south. Pot barley (for soup) was prepared from home-grown barley in a separate mill, but the making of it was a long slow process. Only a bushel could be handled daily.

Another small place marked on the map but no longer in existence is Polneach — "the watering place of the horses". Long ago it was the Cawdor factor's house, and when Robert Burns visited the area and went to Kildrummie, he called on Ballantyne White, the factor living at Polneach.

The Druids gave some interest to Balnaroid, and a stone circle situated in one of the farm fields was regarded as a fine specimen by local authorities, until some labourers building a dyke removed the stones for its foundation. This incident, I am told, occurred during the factor's absence abroad, and on his return he was so annoyed that he made the men replace one stone to mark the spot of the original circle. I note in Bain's *History of Nairnshire* that it served the purpose of a sundial, "just as a tree or post in the same neighbourhood was the clock of the clachan"; and Bain also tells the story of an old man who walked round the stone circle (when it was complete) three times before beginning work, believing that in doing so it would bring him luck.

Brackla Distillery was built in 1812 by a small company of local gentlemen, one of them Captain William Fraser of Fort George, who ultimately became proprietor. He stayed in Brackla House, but I can find little else of interest about this building.

Geddes House was built in 1805 and enlarged twenty-five years later; it was once owned by the Roses of Kilravock.

In fact, old Geddes kirkyard to the east of the house has been the family burying ground of the Roses of Kilravock for the last 700 years.

Nothing now remains of St Mary's Chapel, which stood on the site of the burying ground, though grave-diggers from time to time unearthed stones which quite probably were the chapels foundations. The chapel was founded by the lairds of Kilravock, and at the time of the Reformation a proposal was put forward to make it

Protestant, but nothing ever came of it. The wall around the Kilravock burying ground is comparatively modern.

I visited this wind-swept kirkyard on the brow of a hill, and found the moss-clad tombstones obviously ancient. Outside the north wall of the Kilravock enclosure are the graves of the Mackintoshes of Geddes.

However, until within living memory, the little churchyard on the hill has been the scene of much merriment apart from sorrow, as the former Geddes Markets were held there annually about the 5th April. Vendors of miscellaneous wares displayed their goods on the flat tombstones, while others sat themselves on the headstones of their grandfathers and handed round the whisky glasses.

Near the end of the last century a stop was put to these festivities and the market moved to a more appropriate stance beside the kirkyard.

The name Geddes, incidentally, is believed to have been derived from a British saint, Gildas, who lived in the sixth century.

On the farm of Rait or Raitcastle, we find the ruins of Castle Rait, which was built in the 15th century by Sir Andrew de Rait.

Situated at the foot of Ord Hill, Rait Castle is in some respects almost unique in Scotland. Its shape is oblong with a round tower at the south-west angle, and from the outside has an ecclesiastical appearance. The windows are three feet wide with Gothic arches and mullions. The entrance, some nine feet above the foundations, at the east end of the south wall, still shows the grooves of the portcullis; and the doorway, in the form of an arch was probably protected by a wooden door as the jambs at the sides are still evident. The building was divided into two floors, the bottom without a fireplace.

The tower is said to resemble Edwardian style, and the walls, 5½ feet thick, are made mostly from surrounding rocks. The only complete window is in the tower, but about forty years ago Cawdor estate repaired many of the windows and the entrance way with cement for preservation. The rest of the building stands two storeys high, though it is quite probable that there may have been a third.

I found vestiges of outbuildings surrounding the ruins, and a juniper tree marks the position of a well, probably the castle's main water supply; while the building appears to have been bounded on three sides by a wall, the rocks on the south side forming a natural defence.

36. TRYSTING STONE

The breeding of Clydesdale horses on Cawdor Home Farm was a tradition for many generations until quite recently, when the last of these fine horses found its way to a southern slaughterhouse.

We find Cawdor Home Farm on the south road from the village which takes us into the Nairnshire hills and ultimately on to the Grantown road. But it is difficult for me to describe any definite route, as there are so many distractions on the wayside.

For instance, let us take a small bumpy road almost opposite Cawdor Home Farm, past Balloan and into Culcharry, a small hamlet of little consequence, where we find a collection of houses and a Free Church. It was built in 1849 by the local folk, the farmers supplying free labour.

Within the acreage of Little Urchany are three sites of interest: a Druid circle, a chapel and a burying ground. A stream flowing past the farm is still called Chapel Strip. Nothing is known of the chapel or its burying ground.

Before reaching the village of Rigoul along the Meikle Urchany road, I noticed a large boulder lying in a clump of trees and on enquiry was told that it is the Trysting Stone or Lover's Stone which claims the same story as Croy's Whispering Stone. Being nearer Rait Castle than Croy, I imagine Rigoul's claim is more authentic, because these were the days before pedal cycles were invented!

At one time, it seems, the Cummings of Rait Castle were at enmity with the Mackintoshes of Dalcross, and the family at Rait decided on rather a gruesome plan to murder their foes by inviting them to a banquet, where at a given signal they would be set upon and killed. All members of the Cumming household were sworn to secrecy, but a daughter of the Chief being anxious for the safety of her lover, one of the invited Mackintoshes, arranged to meet him at the stone, where he would hear something of grave importance. Accordingly, the young Mackintosh lad came to the Stone to meet his sweetheart, and crouched down beside it. The girl lay hidden on the other side, and in "a loud whisper" divulged the whole truth of the plot to the Stone, so that her lover could hear all, thus delivering her message without forfeiting her family honour.

However, the Mackintoshes did not refrain from attending the banquet, and at a given signal — the toast to the Memory of the Dead — the Cummings drew their broadswords for attack. But alas! the Mackintoshes rose, daggers in hand, and set upon their assailants, thrusting the daggers into their hearts. Among the few who escaped was the girl's father, who, suspecting the treachery of his daughter, rushed to her room. As he swung open the door the girl realised his maddened state, but before she could attempt to escape by the window the Chief had cut off both her hands with his sword.

From that night, so says tradition, the blood-stained walls of Rait remained tenantless.

Rigoul is very small and consists of a few houses and a school. The derivation is "king's place" which may have had some connection with Castle Finlay nearby, an old vitrified fort protected by ditches and earthworks. Little is known about the castle, but the gentleman who gave his name to the fort is believed to have been Finlay, the father of MacBeth, and both were Kings of Moray.

A hillock, three hundred yards down the Littlemill road, in an Achavraat field is known as Tomnacrochar — hangman's hill — where sheep and cattle stealers met their deaths when the law was a rough and ready affair.

Achavraat marches with New Achamore to the west and Keppernach to the east, and there must be something very special about the latter as the grass in the early summer often seems to be further advanced than on neighbouring holdings. It may be due to better soil.

The story of the soldier's grave at Keppernach has several versions, but the theme is simple. Making his way home to this district from the Battle of Culloden, a wounded soldier succumbed and died in the Keppernach Burn, where he was found and buried by the local folk on a spot now quite near the roadside. All round the little cairn, which marks its position, a new plantation is quickly growing up, but until the First World War it was practically hidden among the trees of an older forest. During that war Canadian troops cleared away the timber, but revered the site of the unknown soldier's grave. Beside it they erected a small notice board, with the words:

"Just to remind, lest we forget
A comrade buried here.
In leisure hours, please gather flowers,
And keep his memory dear."

I am afraid this touching epitaph has long since disappeared, but the natives of Ardclach do not forget. Every generation has tended the grave, and it is seldom without flowers.

37. LOCH OF BOATH

To reach the district of Clunas we branch off the south road from Cawdor at Little Urchany. Before coming to Ordbreck a small rough road forks to the left towards Drumcharrel, and beyond it is the croft of Tomcluag. The name, I am told, means "bell hill' and, according to an old tradition, a bell from Barevan Church was once buried in a hillock on the farm.

The Loch of Boath actually lies behind Balmore, and according to an old story the site of this lakelet was a valuable peat bog. Gradually, as the people removed their peats for winter fuel, the hollow formed filled with water. About 1750 the Cawdor factor decided to drain the loch, and arranged with a local contractor to do the work. But no sooner had the first sod been cut, than the heavens opened and a terrible thunderstorm broke out overhead. The lightning was frightening and ran along the workmen's shovels and picks, till they became thoroughly disheartened. They struck work, and declared that neither lord nor factor would ever make them return to the job again. So the loch has remained! It is also said to be the haunt of a Water Bull, and may be connected by underground channels with Loch Belivat on the other side of the parish.

To the north of Carn an Cailich — the "hill of the old woman or nun" (who is supposed to have lived in a cottage on the east side in Celtic times) — we meet the road from the Meikleburn, a collection of crofts known generally by that name, though individually identified in some instances. All bound the Muckle Burn, and to reach them we must ford the river, usually along some of the worst tracks in the county.

There is Rumachroy — "The red marsh" — with its oozing chalybeate waters, which is worked along with Tachter. The full name of Tachter is Loch-an-Taister-e, meaning the Devil's Loch, but it has long since dried up. Its name had a connection with smuggling, which was fairly rife in the district in past days.

Lubleister has a flavour of Caithness about the name, but is derived from the Gaelic, meaning Lily Marsh. It appears to have been named from the abundance of a curious water plant called seilisdear, which grew in a wet bog beside the house.

38.   THE PRINCESS STONE

The Grantown road branches off the east highway just outside of Nairn, and after passing the burgh cemetery on our right we presently reach Househill. This estate along with Crook belonged to Nairn at one time, and was bought from the burgh by the Roses of Kilravock. About the year 1780, Hugh Rose of Kilravock sold them to Hugh Robertson, a merchant of the town; and since then the properties have changed hands many times.

My ordnance survey map marks a tumulus to the south of Littlemill, but, although I have enquired extensively about its origin and position, nobody seems to know anything about it. However, we cannot fail to see Tom Fade, better known as the Sian or the Fairy Hill. It is just a plain little green hillock with one solitary tree, but according to tradition it is the last place in Nairnshire where fairies were seen to play.

The estate of Glenferness is owned by the Earl of Leven and Melville, a young laird who succeeded to the title a year or two ago on the death of his father. The former site of the House was at Castle Park, but in 1814 the family of Dougals, then proprietors of the estate, decided to demolish the building and rebuilt it on its present site near the River Findhorn.

Until 1938 the house was harled in red, but in that year the harling was removed and the stonework pointed. The house is now a fine stately building.

Down by the river, and almost hidden by undergrowth and shrubbery is the Princess Stone, held in place by two supports. It is a fine monolith covered with descriptive Celtic art; and although now greatly wasted by time, it must have been a very beautiful piece of sculpture.

The story of the Princess Stone takes us back in history to the 10th century or earlier, when the Castle of Lochindorb, now ruined, and situated on a small island in the loch, was an important edifice in the district. In fact, it appears to have been a royal residence, and near it the local forces assembled the night before a battle in the vicinity of Dunearn, to check the invading Norsemen.

Under the leadership of King Fergus, the Moray men gained a complete victory, and captured Prince Harold, the Danish leader. They marched him off to Lochindorb Castle as prisoner and flung him into a dungeon. Soon afterwards the invaders were driven out, and peace reigned over the whole province.

Some time later King Sewyn of Denmark tried to conclude a peace treaty and family alliance by contriving a marriage between his son Hárold, in prison at Lochindorb, and Malvina, King Fergus' only daughter. All the necessary nuptial arrangements were made, but the Prince and Princess were not consulted. The wedding was to be a surprise for them both. However, they had not been altogether idle themselves, and had fallen madly in love, little thinking they would obtain parental consent.

They decided to elope, and on the eve of the public wedding made a secret escape. Taking with them the King's favourite grey horse, they crossed the loch in one of the castle's boats and landed on the northern shore without raising an alarm. They reached the Findhorn to find further progress barred by flooded waters, and meantime took refuge in a small chapel on the eastern side of the Doune of Dunearn. From there they espied the approach of the King's men, and decided that if an escape was possible they must attempt a crossing of the river regardless of the spate.

Mounting the grey steed, they galloped down the hillside, but the wise animal refused to cross until a prick from the Prince's dagger sent horse and lovers struggling and plunging in the river. A day or two later the lovers' bodies were found locked together on the grassy bank a short way from the Mansion of Glenferness.

By order of the royal parents, they were buried on the spot. A stone cairn built up from the pebbles of the river, along with the designed monolith, marked the grave, and later some sympathetic hand, no doubt, planted a birch and rowan trees in memory of these two tragic lovers.

39.   HEIGHT OF THE STONES

The parish of Ardclach is undoubtedly the most interesting district of Nairnshire, and although we have visited some of the places in the parish in the foregoing chapter, we have yet to explore the more central area. The derivation of Ardclach is the "height of the stones". We find them everywhere, hampering cultivations.

Standing on a hill overlooking the old church in the hollow is the famous Ardclach Bell Tower, with the reputation of being the highest belfry in Scotland. But, strange as it may seem, it does not stand on church land. This fact has given rise to the suggestion that the tower was not built for the purpose of heralding people to church, but that it was once an estate prison, and that the Laird of Lethen allowed the Kirk Session to use it as a place of confinement for moral delinquents and later as a bell house.

On approaching the tower, up the stone steps, we find it compactly built. The southern gable has been coped with an open granite belfry, while the other finishes off in an ordinary chimney. Underneath the former is carved the date 1655, but according to an old tradition it is probable that the building is at least the second on the site.

A raiding party from the West, stealing along the bed of the Findhorn, climbed the bank of the river and at the dead of night began their work of destruction. Dismantling the bell from its perch, they stripped all the fittings inside and set the tower ablaze. The bell rolled down the hill, chiming as it tumbled, till it reached the waters of the Findhorn, where it lay at rest. There it might have lain forgotten were we not reminded by the tradition that when the river is in full spate the bell is still heard to chime in muffled tones!

In comparison with some of the meagre acres of Ardclach the green fields of Dulsie suggest different fertility. But he still has plenty of stones to worry about!

The farmhouse of Dulsie is an old Wade roadhouse or inn, and it is said Robert Burns called there in his travels in the north. The hill behind the house, Tom nan.Meann, was ploughed round and round within living memory and cropped until the encroaching heather took over.

An early name for the Findhorn was the Earn, and about a mile from Dulsie Bridge we reach the Doune of Dunearn. It is believed to have been a vitrified fort, but all traces of vitrification have disappeared from the top, at any rate.

Beyond Refouble to the east is Aitnoch, "the place of the junipers", and in the old days the juniper supplied the main fuel for the hearth on this Nairnshire croft. The Hill of Aitnoch is the highest mount in that vicinity.

So we reach the southernmost part of the county, and can find no more traces of habitation. However, officially, the Nairnshire roads travel south a mile or two, and a tiny portion of the boundary with Morayshire scrapes the edges of Lochindorb, introduced into modern fiction by Maurice Walsh in his book, *The Key Above the Door*.

40.   FAIRY PRANKS

Almost midway between Littlemill and Belivat villages, the Jubilee road leads to Lethen. It is not, perhaps, the most direct way of getting there, but one of the several thoroughfares leading east from the Grantown road.

Kronyhillock is a tiny farm on our left, now under the jurisdiction of Lethen estate, and it derives its name from the number of cronies which used to be gathered there. I understand "crony" was a common name given to the tuberous bitter vetch, which grew there in abundance, and was greatly relished by the Highlander. It had a sweet taste, rather like liquorice, and in times of scarcity actually was used as a substitute for bread. The young folks chewed it in the same way their fathers chewed tobacco.

The proper entrance to Remore is from Belivat, but I managed to find a less used track bounded closely by broom and grass-tufted in the centre. In fact, I am often told if there is a bad road in a district I am sure to take it. The track took me through the Bog of Fornighty, or rather the site where the farm of that name once stood. The bog is still very evident and distinguished by the abundance of cotton grass, but I believe most of the arable land is now included within the acreage of Fornighty Farm.

Remore stands on the face of the hill beyond the bog, but I was disappointed not to find any traces of the old meal mill, which, according to tradition, was once haunted by the fairies. At night when the labours of the miller were over, the Little Folk who lived in the recesses of Cairnbar, were said to take over, grind their own fairy corn, then return fully laden to their homes in the hillside.

As time went on, one of these little folk became bolder, and to have everything ready for the midnight activities, he was in the habit of turning up at the mill some time before the miller's departure. Naturally the miller resented the intrusion, especially when, after finishing its work, the creature would sit down at the fire to await the arrival of its companions. One night at his wits' end, the miller took his rake and scattered the burning embers of the fire all over the place, making the little gnome hop furiously about the mill, bewildered and terribly burnt, and screaming in rage and pain.

Presently the mill door flew open, and a multitude of little folk were soon swarming into the mill, shouting for revenge. At last the noise ceased, and the miller had hopes of escape. But his exit was barred, and, gnashing their teeth, the horde advanced towards him.

Just at that moment the cock crowed and the spell was broken; and from that day to this the little folk were never seen again around Remore.

Thousands of years ago the sea is believed to have risen to these heights, and there's an interesting fish fossil quarry at Lethen Bar. The fossils crop up occasionally during cultivations, and specimens are preserved in Nairn Museum and Lethen House. I am told, too, that a plant fossil quarry exists beside Lethen.

The family of Brodie of Lethen is one of the oldest in Nairnshire, and representatives of this family feature in the county's history throughout the generations. However, the early history of the Brodies is rather vague due to the destruction of family papers, but they are believed to be of Celtic origin. We find one present at the reconciliation in 1380 of the Wolf of Badenoch; another took part in the Battle of the Park, near Contin, in the next century.

The Brodies did not come to Lethen until 1634, when the estate was sold to Alexander Brodie, the first laird of Lethen and second son to Alexander Brodie, the first laird of Lethen and second son of a son of a Brodie of Brodie. Lethen was previously occupied by Falconers since 1295. They sold it to John Grant of Freuchy in 1600, who, it is recorded, built a large house at Lethen, which appears to have been a place of great strength.

The year 1645 was a memorable year in the history of Nairnshire, when, in February, Montrose made one of his sudden dashes into the Northern Highlands and appeared on the border of Moray. His men pillaged the land causing great destruction, and though the House of Lethen was spared, the lands were greatly wasted. Brodie of Lethen was a strong Covenanter. After the battle of Auldearn, Lethen was besieged again, this time by Huntly and his troops, for a period of twelve weeks, and only retired after receiving a promise from Brodie that a bond of money would be made payable to him in case Lethen and his friends did not conform to His Majesty's service.

Some of the walls of the old house of Lethen are incorporated into the present mansion built in 1788 or thereabouts.

At the Moyness cross-roads we find a Stone Circle, with one prominent standing stone. A number of years ago it held a rocking stone on top, which was used in olden times as an ordeal stone for proving the guilt of criminals. The culprit was placed on it, and if the stone rocked, guilt was established. If not, innocence was proved. The rocking stone ultimately split, and its parts are lying on the ground.

Beside Moyness farm steading is the site of the old Castle of Moyness, visited by Mary Queen of Scots in 1562 on her way to Inverness. Although the ruins of Moyness have practically disappeared, it seems to have been a castle of considerable strength, with round towers and surrounding walls. It stood on a ridge commanding a wide view.

41. AULDEARN

Modern Auldearn amounts to little, but, historically speaking, it really is interesting. For instance, it was the official seat of the Dean of the Diocese of Moray, and part of the old kirk, now roofless, still stands in the local burying ground.   The church used to be one of those old-fashioned churches with the pulpit in the middle, and the galleries all round it, but it was gutted out in comparatively recent times and reconditioned.

The kirk of Auldearn stands boldly on a height with the village nestling below, and it was erected in 1757, when the former building was burnt. Until their own private burying ground was opened, the Brodies of Lethen had their family vault within the north end of the kirk. In the churchyard are the graves of several Covenanters who bravely died at the Battle of Auldearn.

The present village is gradually being extended, and although the main street "runs" east to west and is bordered by houses, it originally occupied a different situation and lay north to south. Indeed this was the lie of the land at the time of the Battle of Auldearn fought in 1645 between the Covenanters and Montrose's army.

The Covenanters, under the command of General Hurry, had fallen back to Inverness, and Montrose pitched camp at Auldearn, making the House of Boath his headquarters. His position was strong, and in setting up his forces he took full advantage of the natural defences of the ground. Concentrating his main forces on the left wing, commanded by Lord Lewis Gordon, somewhere in the vicinity of Newmill, he drew up his command along the ridge where the road now passes. He also made use of the Doocot Hill to place a few picket musketeers with cannon.

The plan of the battle was most skilfully laid, the object being to draw the best fighting regiments of the Covenanters to attack the centre of the column, commanded by Major-General Alexander MacDonald, while the left wing would swoop down during that engagement.

Now when MacDonald — sometimes known as Colkitto — was arranging his defences by camouflaging his ranks with brushwood, a message was handed to him from Lord Gordon on the left flank. It read:

"Allaster MacDonald, I have heard that there was a bond of friendship between our forefathers, not to strike a blow against each other, whatever quarrel might be between them and the rest of Scotland, and none excelled them in deeds of honour; therefore, let us now renew that bond by exchanging foot soldiers on this the first day of my doing battle for my King — send me your foot soldiers and take mine."

The flattered General at once agreed, and ordered ninety of his best men to be transferred to his friend, who in return sent 300 of his inexperienced soldiers, which he was only too willing to lose. MacDonald was left with fifty veterans of his own, and had to place them, half in front and half behind the Gordon recruits to keep them from running away.

Shortly before noon on the 9th May 1645, the Battle of Auldearn commenced. Part of the Covenanting army, under Loudon and Lawrie, with trained veterans, followed the line of the Kinnudie Burn and attacked MacDonald's flank. But the cavalry could not charge, due to the boggy nature of the ground. MacDonald's position was fairly secure behind the brushwood. It infuriated his enemy, who retorted with gibes that the Major-General was a coward.

Montrose had ordered MacDonald not to leave his position, but the gibes hurt deep, and he sallied forth with his raw recruits to meet the Covenanters in the open. A fierce battle ensued, but the Gordons would not fight and ducked their heads at flying arrows and shot. Their officers had to shoot many to prevent flight.

MacDonald was forced back, fighting step by step, and he was the last man to seek the protection of the enclosures.

Montrose watched the battle from the churchyard, and on hearing that MacDonald had disobeyed orders and was being routed, he shouted an encouragement to Lord Gordon:

"MacDonald is gaining the victory single-handed! Come, come, my Lord Gordon, shall he carry all before him and leave no laurels for the house of Huntly? Charge!"

Just at that moment, Major Drummond on the Covenanting side was also ordered to charge, but for some inexplicable reason he broke through the infantry ranks behind him and made off. An ideal opportunity for Montrose's men to enter the confusion, and presently the coventanters were being mown down like grass. Montrose's victory was complete.

Two hundred years ago Boghole was an important ecclesiastical centre in the county. Built in 1753, the church came under the rule of the Secession Church, and the congregation was united with the Seceders of Morayshire. About the middle of the 18th century the minister was Henry Clark, and it was during his ministry that those members living in and around Nairn wanted to build a separate church in the town. In 1759, three elders and sixty-one members applied to be disjoined from Boghole and formed into a separate congregation, on the understanding that public worship was to be conducted in Gaelic only. The Boghole congregation strongly objected on the ground that the preaching of Gaelic in Nairn would affect the attendance at Boghole; so a compromise was agreed upon, that the preaching of Gaelic must not come nearer than Balblair, a mile west of Nairn. The Gaelic speakers worshipped here for about a year, but still the Boghole congregation was dissatisfied, and they had to move farther away. Finally, they settled at Howford.

We are now bordering on Morayshire, and from Boghole we eventually join the main Nairn—Forres road at the Hardmuir. A little to the east of Easter Hardmuir is MacBeth's Hillock, where tradition says he met the weird witches on the Blasted Heath.

About a mile east of Nairn, past Achnacloich, we sidetrack towards Inshoch, and the first few cottages we approach have the famous name of Waterloo. The explanation I received locally was that some Irishmen used to stay in them and fought among themselves so much that the place won its name. The cottages are now attached to Achnacloich for farm workers.

The House of Boath is a square, two-storeyed building, built for Captain Sir James Dunbar by Archibald Simpson of Aberdeen in 1827. It has been described as the most beautiful Regency house in Scotland. The Dunbars lived in it until 1923, when they sold it to Admiral Sir Heathcote Grant. After his death Lady Grant sold the estate, and during the last war the old house was requisitioned by the army, who left it in disreputable condition.

On the rising ground in front of a former Boath House, Montrose waited with his army for the approaching Covenanters. A well, about seventy yards in front of the dining-room window, is known locally as Montrose's Well. Doocot Hill with its old dovecot may have been a moot hill many centuries ago, but later became the site of a tower or castle.

Lochloy is separated from the shore by a marsh, now partly planted, and I notice that birches have grown profusely in this area. Many years ago a village existed, and last century a number of hearthstones, querns and other bits of homes were dug up. There's the site of an old chapel and a graveyard, too. A chapel well is supposed to have healing qualities.

The village had a port, and about three-quarters of a mile eastwards another village was Maviston. The fishermen, it is believed, used the Lochloy port for their boats, while they resided at Maviston.

The only remaining evidence today of a fishing population exists in the few bothies we find dotted around this coast. These are at

West Bar, Shallow Head and the Hillocks, and at Kingsteps. An ice-house is built into the hillside, where the fishermen stored ice collected from a nearby loch (now practically dried up on the Golf Links) in preparation for the salmon fishing season. Each bothy had its ice-house, comparable with the modern refrigerator.

42. HISTORY IN MOY

I am rather ashamed of myself. I was beginning to think that the link between clansmen and their chiefs was breaking and that Scots were no longer clan chief conscious. I was wrong, as I found out when I visited Moy Hall, the home of The Mackintosh of Mackintosh.

The original home of the Mackintosh chiefs was built on an island on Loch Moy in the 14th century, and the last building sited there was burned down in the 18th century.

The present Hall was built about 1800, the central portion being the oldest, and other parts were added seventy years later. It is an exceptionally fine building of grey granite.

Perhaps the best known story about the Mackintoshes is the Rout of Moy. Lady Mackintosh, by birth Anne Farquharson, was a Jacobite at heart, though her husband served in the Government Army. On the 16th February 1746, Prince Charles was staying at Moy Hall, as guest of Lady Mackintosh, when a youth brought news of a strong detachment of Government troops approaching, under the command of Lord Loudon, to seize the Prince. It was obvious that they would easily outnumber the Moy bodyguard, so Lady Mackintosh told the local blacksmith, a Fraser, to gather all the men he could muster and oppose them. But men were scarce, and taking the handful he could find, he posted them at various points on the old Inverness road. As the soldiers approached, the blacksmith shouted out to his stalwarts, calling on the MacDonalds and the Camerons, and mentioning Keppoch and Lochiel by name, as if he was in command of the whole Highland army. The ruse worked, and soon the Hanoverians were fleeing in haste back the way they had come.

However, a volley from the little band of Jacobites killed one man — the great MacCrimmon, King of Pipers, who, it is thought, against his will had joined his clan in the Government forces.

The old Inverness road does not follow the track of the present highway, and I am told that the Rout of Moy actually took place at the back of the hill near the farm of Ault-na-Slanach ("the burn of health").

The village of Moy is a small scattered community, and perhaps of most interest in it is the parish church. It lies slightly behind the manse. It dates back to 1760, when it was built by Rev. James Leslie, a giant in stature, who was said to be nearer seven feet tall than six. But according to some of the tales told about him, I gather he was none too popular. On one occasion he went over to Dalarossie to preach, and at Auchintoul was met by a band of angry women, who threatened him with stones. He managed to dissuade them from doing him bodily harm by calling out:

"Let the first witch of you throw the first stone."

Not one did!

The scenery along Loch Moy is exquisite, especially with autumn tints, and on the larger of two islands, an obelisk has been erected to the memory of Sir Aeneas Mackintosh, twenty-third chief, who died in 1829.

Near Moy School a cattle tryst was held long ago, and its site is still marked by a stone; but these markets ceased to function after the murder of two travellers on the wayside there in 1720. The markets continued to be held on a piece of ground now flanked by the road and railway, about a quarter of a mile on the Moy side of Dalmagarry.

Tullochclury lies well back from the road, and the farmhouse was the first to be slated in the district, when it was tenanted by the estate factor. Years ago a school was in use beside it.

The farmhouse of Dalmagarry was built as an inn in 1732 by The Mackintosh, and part of it — an old style black kitchen — was burnt at the time of Culloden. The sheiling nearby, once the stables, was burned too.

Taking the Shenachie road beyond Dalmagarry, we follow the Moy Burn and come to the deserted house of Milton of Moy, with the ruins of a meal mill. The machinery of the mill was disposed of as scrap during the last war, but there has not been a miller in it since Lewes Rose, Ruthven, retired in 1921. The former name of Milton is Culfintack.

Achandalan ("field of the flood of beer") is a 'keeper's house built prominently on the summit of a brae, and the two farms of Ruthven lie on the green haughs on the banks of the Findhorn. At one time Ruthven was a fair-sized community, and the ruins of at least seven holdings can still be seen.

The Freeburn Hotel is a very attractive place, especially for the angler and folk wanting a quiet restful holiday. The River Findhorn is famous for its brown trout and salmon. The climate is bracing as Tomatin is 1000 feet above sea-level. The hotel was built about 1814, and until the beginning of this century a cattle market was held in a field in front of it. Across the burn, beside the hotel, the Grants from Strathspey set up their own stances to sell animals and produce. These markets followed on the old Dalmagarry markets.

At one time it seems, Freeburn was part of a small estate owned by Mackintosh of Holme and known as the Free estate. It was not very large, stretching between the Alt-dub-hag ("wee black burn") and the Free Burn. The farm of Free has been taken over by the Tomatin Distillery Company, and built on it now are several fine houses. At a bend in the road near Sandside, a toll gate blocked the thoroughfare years ago, until it was removed and used in one of the Free Farm cattle-folds.

The position of Tomatin Distillery in many respects is ideal. Plenty of water from the Free Burn, peat from the hillsides and the convenience of the railway are valuable assets. It was built in 1897.

Before the introduction of motor traffic, Tomatin was a popular health resort and continued so until about 1910.

We fork left at the road sign "Balvraid", pass under the railway viaduct, and then cross the River Findhorn by a wooden-decked iron bridge. It is the third bridge on record. A three-arch one, built about 1760, was swept away in the 1829 flood, and a "temporary" bridge put in its place was carried away by ice about a hundred years later. The present one was built about 1879. It cost £1000; local lairds supplying the material, crofters and others doing the work. The other bridges, however, were located farther down-stream, where Wade's road approached it.

On the far side of the bridge we come to a "T" bend, and at the junction of the Balvraid and Soilshan roads is a stone-built memorial erected by the people of Strathdearn and Inverness shooting friends to the memory of Rev. Edwin Leece Browne, M.A., St Andrew's School, Eastbourne, who, for fifty years, was shooting tenant at Glenkirk. He died in 1933.

I climbed Wade's road to the school with its schoolhouse dating back to Culloden. It is believed to have been standing during the battle. The derivation of Raigbeg is "small circle", in this case a burying ground, as it was a custom to make such places in that form. Also in the Tomatin district is Raigmore — "the big circle", similarly a burying ground.

On the brae face below Edinchat the Bruachaig Burn has gradually seeped away much of the embankment, especially during spates, and a flood from Loch Bruachaig in 1923 destroyed the greater part of the arable land around the burn, leaving it marshy and full of rushes. The same flood accounted for part of Balnespick Lodge garden and removed a section of the gardener's house.

This is a lonely countryside, 'midst heather-clad hills. The crofters have known no other life, but have won fame through their sheep. Those who remain in this small fraternity are hardy folk, making a living through work and thrift, and envy no other way of life.